W9-CES-562

Words, Words, Words

vocabularies and dictionaries

HAYDEN ENGLISH LANGUAGE SERIES

Robert W. Boynton — Consulting Editor

*Former Principal, Senior High School
and Chairman, English Department
Germantown Friends School*

AN INTRODUCTION TO MODERN ENGLISH GRAMMAR
J. Malmstrom

LANGUAGE IN SOCIETY (Rev. 2nd Ed.)
J. Malmstrom

WORDS, WORDS, WORDS:
Vocabularies and Dictionaries (Rev. 2nd Ed.)
R. Lodwig and E. Barrett

WRITING TO BE READ
K. Macrorie

TELLING WRITING
K. Macrorie

ENGLISH I and II: A Contemporary Approach
R. W. Boynton, R. Johnson, and R. Reeves

WORKOUTS IN READING AND WRITING
O. B. Davis

Words, Words, Words

vocabularies and dictionaries

Revised Second Edition

(Formerly, The Dictionary and the Language)

RICHARD R. LODWIG
Instructor of English
Benson High School, Portland, Oregon

EUGENE F. BARRETT
Coordinator, Communications Division
Cascade Center, Portland Community College
Portland, Oregon

HAYDEN BOOK COMPANY, INC.
Rochelle Park, New Jersey

ISBN 0-8104-5054-2 (soft-bound edition)
        0-8104-5055-0 (hard-bound edition)
Library of Congress Catalog Card Number 73-7000
Copyright © 1967, 1973

The First Edition of this volume was published under the title *The Dictionary and the Language.*

1 2 3 4 5 6 7 8 9 PRINTING

73 74 75 76 77 78 YEAR

Preface

This is a book about words and their meanings. It is also a book about the dictionary and about lexicography, the art and science of dictionary making. These topics are unified to provide a comprehensive text for English language studies and for vocabulary development. The three major elements—words, meanings, and the dictionary—form a happy partnership, reinforcing and complementing each other, since one cannot study words and meanings for long without reaching for the dictionary, nor can one learn about the dictionary without becoming involved with words and meanings.

This is not a book of picturesque word origins, nor is it a standard treatment of "dictionary skills"—although both ideas may appear in appropriate places. Instead, it is a word-centered approach to language, an attempt to teach the student about the growth and development of his native tongue. By the time that he has read and worked his way through the text, the student should know a great deal about the English language and may be intellectually excited about what he has discovered. He will certainly realize, perhaps for the first time, that it is a living, growing, changing, exciting language.

The first half of the text is primarily about the words in our language—native words, borrowed words and the historical background of word borrowing, the creation of new words, word meaning, and changes in word meaning.

In the second half of the text the emphasis is upon the dictionary, the repository of the English vocabulary—its development, its growth into the modern dictionary with its many specialized forms, modern lexicographical theory and practice, the conflict between modern theory and public attitudes, and the efficient use of the dictionary both for language research and for everyday matters.

Vocabulary development is a major concern in this text. Teachers generally recognize that there is no easy road to vocabulary enrichment, that vocabulary workbooks and other "vocabulary programs" are so artificial and limited in their approaches that they fail to effect significant carry-over after a particular batch of words has been "covered."

We have taken a different approach. Throughout the book the student is given many opportunities for vocabulary enrichment. As he learns about language, he is also shown the variety of methods by which word understanding occurs, and as he does the exercises in the text, he practices these methods. Moreover, since the dictionary is a primary resource, a necessary companion to the text, the student should be an expert user of the dictionary by the time he has finished.

But our most important vocabulary aid is the subject matter of the book itself. Quite frankly, we expect that it will make the student so aware of, so interested in, and so knowledgeable about words that he will look upon them perceptively long after the text is out of print. His vocabulary development will then take care of itself each time he takes up a book.

More exercises have been provided for writing, discussion, and reinforcement of learning than most classes can cover conveniently. We suggest that they be reviewed in advance by the teacher, who can then decide which will be most valuable to use in the available time. The teacher may also want to shorten particular assignments as well.

We recognize that many English classes may not have easy access to abundant reference works, and we have planned our exercises accordingly. We expect, however, that the student will occasionally be able to consult an unabridged dictionary in the classroom or school library, and certainly that each student will have the use in class of a good college-edition desk dictionary. Under ideal conditions, a classroom might contain the following valuable materials to supplement the text:

1. A classroom set of desk dictionaries. We recommend these as being especially suitable: *Webster's New World Dictionary*, second edition, *The Random House Dictionary*, *The American Heritage Dictionary*, *Webster's Seventh New Collegiate Dictionary*, and the *Standard College Dictionary*. For purposes of comparison, at least one copy of each of the titles listed should be available.

2. Two unabridged dictionaries. We recommend *Webster's Third New International Dictionary* and either *The Random House Dictionary of the English Language* or Funk and Wagnalls' *The New Standard Dictionary*.

3. *Dictionaries and That Dictionary*, by James Sledd and Wilma R. Ebbitt (Chicago: Scott, Foresman and Company, 1962). This book reprints many of the reviews which appeared following the publication of *Webster's Third New International Dictionary*.

4. *Johnson's Dictionary, A Modern Selection*, by E. L. McAdam, Jr. and George Milne (New York: Pantheon Books, 1963).

5. *Dictionary of American Slang*, by Harold Wentworth and S. B. Flexner (New York: Thomas Y. Crowell Co., 1967).

6. Two synonym reference books. We recommend *Thesaurus of English Words and Phrases*, by Peter Mark Roget (New York: Thomas Y. Crowell Co., 1946), and *Webster's Dictionary of Synonyms* (Springfield: G. and C. Merriam Co., 1942).

7. Two books of English usage. We recommend *Current American Usage*, by Margaret Bryant (New York: Funk and Wagnalls Company, 1962), and *A Dictionary of Modern English Usage*, by H. W. Fowler, second edition, revised by Sir Ernest Gowers (New York: Oxford University Press, 1965). Here is an opportunity to compare American usage with that of our British cousins.

8. Three books which describe the history and development of the language. We suggest *History of the English Language*, by Albert C. Baugh (New York: Appleton-Century-Crofts, Inc., 1958), *The Development of Modern English*, by Stuart Robertson and Frederic G. Cassidy (Englewood Cliffs, N. J.: Prentice-Hall, Inc., 1954), and *The American Language*, by H. L. Mencken, in the one-volume abridged edition by Raven I. McDavid, Jr., with the assistance of David W. Maurer (New York: Alfred A. Knopf, Inc., 1963).

RICHARD R. LODWIG
EUGENE F. BARRETT

Contents

1

Words

1. What Is a Word?

What is a word? A difficult question. Charlton Laird, an eminent scholar and expert on language, says that even the lexicographer (dictionary maker) has a difficult time deciding: ". . . although he assumes he must organize his book on the basis of words, he does not know what a word is, and nobody at this date will tell him." Even experts, suggests Laird, do not agree on all points of definition.

Many people tend to think of a word in visual terms, that is, as a meaningful group of letters printed or written horizontally across a piece of paper. Such a casual conception, of course, is little more than a reflection of the millions of words which roll off printing presses and into our consciousness on pages of newspapers, magazines, and books.

But it is also true as well that serious students of language have long considered the word *as written* to be their chief concern. For the etymologist, the historian of words, it is almost his only concern. (As for the *spoken* language, it is of interest to him only insofar as changes in word forms have been brought about in the past by changing patterns of speech.) For the philologist, as a student of language in literature, the spoken word is in the last analysis spoken only in print and is thus inseparable from the written word. Even linguists, scholars who deal with the spoken word in

1

all its aspects, have traditionally depended on the written word as primary source material for defining the essential meanings of words.

There is an increasingly prominent school of linguists, however, who insist that if one wants to have the last word about words—their current *real* meaning and significance—the study of the spoken word is vastly more important than the study of the written. Children learn to master the sounds of a language, its basic grammatical structure and an elementary vocabulary, long before they learn to write. And historically, the spoken word comes first. The earliest evidence of writing dates back only about six thousand years, but estimates of how long man has been speaking one language or another range from fifty thousand to several hundred thousand years.

What is a word, then, as defined in terms of spoken language? Linguists talk about a word in the following scientific ways:

1. It is a sound or combination of sounds which we make voluntarily with our vocal equipment. (One could argue about whether the words one says after hitting a thumb with a hammer are voluntarily or involuntarily induced.) Not every language uses exactly the same set of sounds to form words. In English, the units of sounds, called "phonemes," are made up of twenty-four consonants and nine vowels. When linguists symbolize these sounds in writing, they use a special phonemic alphabet that has a different symbol for each phoneme. These symbols are written between slanting lines, in the following fashion, to let the reader know that they do not indicate merely letters:

/æ/	(the vowel in *black, mat, bang*)
/ŝ/	(the first sound in *shirt* and the last in *flash*)
/ey/	(the diphthong in *say, hate, same*)
/ə/	(the vowel called schwa, in *run, flood,* and both syllables of *among*)
/ŋ/	(the last consonant sound in *running*)
/j/	(the first sound in *jazz* and the last in *bridge*)

Since our regular twenty-six-letter alphabet is insufficient to cover each of the thirty-three phonemes with a separate symbol, one can see why a phonemic alphabet is necessary if sounds are to be recorded accurately.

In addition to the thirty-three phonemes, three other sound characteristics of our language have been identified: stress, pitch, and juncture. Stress has to do with the degree of loudness, or accent, which is given to certain words or parts of words. Pitch refers to voice tones, which may range from high to low in a typical utterance. Juncture has to do with the pauses between speech sounds and at the end of utterances and also with the things that happen to the voice tones at those times. As a simple illustration, notice how these characteristics help clarify the meaning of the following sentences when they are spoken aloud:

I want some whitewall paint   (paint for my tires)
I want some white wall paint   (paint for my living room)

In writing, the space or lack of it between *white* and *wall* helps us understand what is intended. In speech, our use of stress, pitch, and juncture does the job. Some linguists classify stress, pitch, and juncture into twelve levels and characteristics. These "suprasegmental phonemes," as they are called, have also been assigned special visual symbols.

Phonemes, which are the smallest working units of sound *per se*, build up into morphemes, which are the smallest working units of meaningful sound. A morpheme is composed of one or more phonemes. For example:

Morphemes, or meaning units	Phonemes, or pure sound units	
I	/ay/	(one unit)
hat	/hæt/	(three units)
gem	/jem/	(three units)
sludge	/sləj/	(four units)

A morpheme may be a complete word (*boy*); it may be a word form such as an affix (*-able, in-, -hood*); or it may be a combining form (*bio-, geo-, ped-*). Sometimes its significance is only grammatical. Notice:

girl (one morpheme)   girls (two morphemes, *girl* and the affix *-s*)

Morphemes which can function by themselves as words are called *free*, as with *baseball* or *hideout*, each of which is composed of two free morphemes. Those which have meaning when connected only to another morpheme are called *bound,* as with the *-or* suffix of *actor* or the *intra-* prefix in *intramural.*

2. A second major characteristic of a word is that it is symbolic: it stands for something else. Each of the world's cultures has come to agree that certain sounds will represent certain objects, happenings, or ideas. The symbolic connection is almost always arbitrary; in other words, there is no logical relationship between the sound which stands for a thing or idea and the actual thing or idea itself. We don't call a bull a *bull,* for example, because either the sound or structure of the four letters that make up the word just automatically suggests the animal in question. It is only a symbolic connection, and the word for a bull might just as reasonably be *lub* or *ulb* if we all agreed that it should be. In Spanish, remember, it's *toro*; in German, it's *Stier.* (Those few words whose sound *does* suggest their sense are called "onomatopoetic" or "echoic" words, imitative sounds such as *buzz* and *tinkle.*)

Words are enormously flexible in function. They can symbolize something right before our eyes in the immediate here and now. They can also symbolize something not present, not seen, and not in immediate experience. They allow us to talk about something which now exists only in our mind, something which has happened in the past, or something which may happen in the future. In these respects human language differs from the call system of animals, who make and respond only to a limited kind and number of sounds, relating only to an immediate and limited situation. As one linguist has observed, a dog can be taught to bark when it is time for his dinner to be placed in front of him, but he can never talk about what he had for dinner the night before.

3. A third major characteristic of a word has to do with its *function;* it helps human beings interact culturally with one another —which is another way of saying "communicate." Words do much more than promote the exchange of information and ideas. As members of society we need words for all our life activities: to show affection, anger, pleasure, fear, and all the other emotions; to persuade others; to make a living; to change our institutions; to uphold law and order; to build dams; to make friends—in short, to operate

normally in terms of our own culture. Without words there could be no culture; they are the glue that holds a society together.

Words help us fulfill the social need of talking together. Often the fact that we are saying *something* is more important than *what* we say. When we meet, we say "How do you do?" without really expecting a physical report; we say "It's a nice day" without wishing really to engage in a meteorological discussion. These customary polite exchanges are a kind of indirect communication. They say, in effect: "I'm being friendly. I anticipate that you will be the same." Thus, words are part of the face we wear when we meet the world.

4. Finally, words are part of the large communication system we call language. A word is partly dependent for meaning upon its use in that larger context. To know a word is to know it in several ways: first, to recognize its sound in the stream of speech; second, to recognize the accumulated experiences with which the sound is associated; third, to recognize its function in a sentence or utterance as it works grammatically with other words.

The instant recognition of word sounds becomes an unconscious mechanical function as one learns to use a language. The instant recognition of meanings is a bit trickier, since one must automatically consider the context of each word in its sentence or utterance, not just the word by itself. *Bull*, for instance, may suggest any one of a number of things, depending upon one's own personal experience of the various meanings the word has previously acquired—the papal bull that is signed by a Pope, the bull that chased Paul Newman in *Butch Cassidy and the Sundance Kid*, the prizefighter in the ring "bulling" his opponent into the ropes, or even the interjection one may snort when told something obviously untrue. In other words, the word *bull* needs other words with it to give it context and pin its meaning down.

A word receives some of its meaning as it fills grammatical slots in a sentence: as subject (The bull chased him), as object (He signed the bull), as verb (Let's bull our way into the line), and as modifier (We had a bull session). It should also be noted that some words—prepositions like *by*, *at*, *of*; conjunctions like *and*, *but*; and so forth—are almost impossible to assign any meaning to without talking about their sentence function.

2. Pronunciation

Pronunciation is flexible. Not only do different speakers pronounce the same word in various ways (*nausea: nô′shə, nô′zi ə, nô′zhə,* etc.), but even a single speaker may give the same word two different pronunciations: "He puts a quarter in the *cigarette′* machine [accent on the last syllable] but didn't get any *cig′arettes* [accent on the first syllable]." Pronunciation may vary from person to person, situation to situation, or place to place for several reasons. For one thing, each person has his own "idiolect," or personal way of speaking, and it varies in subtle ways from every other individual's speech. Norman Hoss, an editor of *The American Heritage Dictionary,* maintains that if analysis were pressed far enough it could be shown that no two Americans speak exactly alike. As a matter of fact, the existence of voiceprints seems to reinforce his statement. Voiceprints are distinctive patterns of wavy lines and whorls which are recorded on a device activated by the human voice. Like fingerprints, they can be used for identification purposes and are even beginning to be accepted as evidence in certain courts of law.

Regional dialects account for many obvious variations in pronunciation. It is easy to recognize, for example, that many people in the New England area put an *r* sound at the end of words like *idea* but leave it out of words like *far, park,* and *four.* Or that some New Yorkers start the second word of *Long Island* with a hard *g* sound (*lôn gi′land*) and put a second syllable in *film* (*fil′əm*).

One of the more important variations in pronunciation happens when words are run together in the stream of speech. One thing that can occur was shown in the example above with *cigarette:* the grammatical position of a word in an utterance may change its syllable stress. A few words in the language always change stress from noun to verb use: *progress′* (*v.*) and *prog′ress* (*n.*), *reject′* (*v.*) and *re′ject* (*n.*), and so forth.

Other things happen also as words follow one another rapidly in speech. Their pronunciation is influenced to some degree by three characteristics previously mentioned: stress, pitch, and juncture. Depending upon particular speech patterns, sounds normally heard when the word is said in isolation may change their values or even disappear as they merge with the sounds which precede or follow them. For instance, when spoken by themselves, or very slowly and deliberately, the italicized words in the following sentences would approximate most of the sounds represented by their spellings:

> See *you bye and bye.*
> I *could have* gone yesterday.
> They believe in *law and order.* -
> I *used to* like spinach.
> *What are you going to* do now?
> *How would you like to* eat dinner now?

But in the normal context of speech the pronunciations for many people would be closer to this:

> See *ya bye n bye.*
> I *could uv* gone yesterday.
> They believe in *law n order.*
> I *use ta* like spinach.
> *What cha gonna do* now?
> *How ja like ta* eat dinner now?

Even finer distinctions can be made.. For instance, a subtle blending takes place in the sounds represented by the *w's*, *t's* and *m's* when combinations like *how would, can't take,* and *I'm making* occur in the stream of speech.

Many writers have fun in print with examples of pronunciation like those above, implying that because the sounds do not conform to the spelling of the written language they are necessarily sloppy speech. But they forget, or do not know, that speech and writing are two separate systems and each has its own special characteristics. There is no law, grammatical or otherwise, that says the sounds of speech must conform to spelling rules; actually, it would be more logical to reverse the order, since writing is a representation of the spoken word, and not vice versa. True, there are always individual variations in speech, depending upon the personal background of the speaker and the formality or informality of the situation. Naturally, when speaking formally or before an audience, pronunciation may be more deliberate, and hence closer to the way the word is said in isolation. But nearly everyone, including the best-educated speakers, follows normal patterns like "could uv

gone" and "law n order" in relaxed speech. Note how the pronunciation entries in *Webster's New World Dictionary, Second Edition*
take these variations into account:

> **and** (ənd, n, 'n, 'm; *stressed,* and)
> **have** (hav, həv, əv; *before "to,"* haf)
> **de-** (di, də; with some slight stress, dē)

An interesting but minor phenomenon is "spelling pronunciation." It is possible to overreact or to react mistakenly to the spelling of a word and give it a pronunciation it does not have normally
in speech (like sounding the *l* in *salmon*). If enough people do this,
of course, the pronunciation becomes acceptable and eventually
supersedes the old pronunciation or exists side by side with it.
Soldier used to be pronounced with the *l* silent (*so'jur*), but in time
the *l* became voiced, probably because people kept seeing it so
often in print. For a more modern example of a spelling pronunciation, consider how you pronounce the work *tsk* when you read it.
(*Tsk* is the repeated sucking or clicking noise made by the tongue
and teeth to express disapproval or sympathy.) If you pronounce
it as *tisk* or *tusk*, as many do when reading it in print, it's because
the written symbols have been inadequate to convey the clicking
sound it actually represents, so a new spelling pronunciation has
been created.

What is good pronunciation? It should be intelligible, natural,
and unobtrusive; that is, it should not call attention to itself. One
can speak too fast and slur sounds until whole sentences become
unrecognizable. When that happens one is speaking "Slurvian," a
foreign dialect as far as standard speech is concerned.

On the other hand it is possible to be over-correct, especially if
one is unduly influenced by the printed symbol. Some radio and
TV announcers read their copy as though they want each letter in
a word to have its "true" hearing. Note these examples which have
been collected from the airwaves: *əprē'sē āt* instead of *əprē'shē āt*,
i'syoo instead of *ish'oo*, *nā'tyoor* instead of *nā'chər*, *ed'yoo kāt* instead of *ej'yoo kāt*, *kwes'tē yən* (three syllables) instead of *kwes'
chən*, *wur'ənt* (two syllables) instead of *wurnt*, and likewise
ar'ənt instead of *arnt*. Pronunciations like these call attention to
themselves and are more apt to sound amusing than impressive.

3. Spelling

Obviously, orthography (spelling) and phonology (pronunciation) do not always agree. One reason for this is that we are working with an alphabet, adopted from the Romans, which does not have a separate letter to represent each sound in the language so that some letters must do double duty or work together in combination. For another reason, when we borrowed words from other languages —French, Latin, and Greek, particularly—we borrowed spellings as well, spellings which were often inconsistent with our own spelling system.

A third reason is that our pronunciation has changed more rapidly than our spelling over the years; in some cases the two have drawn far apart. In bygone days it did not matter much whether a word was spelled in one or in several ways. People were not so used to seeing words in print, and the ideal of spelling uniformity had not been formulated. Records of Shakespeare's time contain over-eighty different spellings of his name, we are told. In fact he often spelled it in different ways himself. Early printers sometimes changed the spelling of words merely to make a line of type come out even. Under conditions like these, spelling could change rather easily to conform to changes in speech.

However, as printing became well established, it had the effect of helping to freeze the spelling of words. We became used to seeing a word as it was spelled and thinking of the printed word as *the* word. Once spelling became standardized, it became sacred. Dictionaries did their share in stopping spelling changes. When the stamp of authority became attached to dictionary pronouncements, spelling changes became difficult to bring about. From time to time, well-meaning groups and individuals like Noah Webster and George Bernard Shaw have tried to reform our orthography, but with little success.

Shaw once announced that he had found a new way to spell the word *fish*. If one used the irregularities of English spelling, he implied, *fish could* be spelled as *ghoti*. Like this:

> *gh* like the *f* in *laugh*
> *o* like the *i* in *women*
> *ti* like the *sh* in *nation*

Shaw's little joke underlines the popular notion we have about our spelling system—that it is an unmanageable, disorganized mess. And to prove it we point to well-publicized boobytraps like *though, cough, tough, bough, through,* and *hiccough*—each spelled exactly alike in the last four letters but pronounced completely differently.

But the truth is that in spite of occasional irregularities such as these, at least eighty percent of our words fit consistent spelling patterns. And even those spellings that appear to be irregular may have more regularity and usefulness than we realize.

For example, "silent letters," those apparently pointless additions to a word, may come alive when a base word is extended into a longer one. Note what happens to the silent letters in the following:

Silent letter in base word	Audible letter in extended word
sign	signify
malign	malignant
hymn	hymnal
phlegm	phlegmatic
condemn	condemnation
bomb	bombard

And silent *-e* at the end of a word is useful in several ways. For one thing, it is a clue to the pronunciation of a preceding vowel. Notice how the *-e* or lack of it on the end of these words tell you how to pronounce them:

din, dine   can, cane   hop, hope   cut, cute

For another, it also tells us how the word will be spelled when certain suffixes are added to it. For example, *-ing* and *-d* added to words ending in silent *-e* produce these spellings:

cane	caning	caned
dine	dining	dined
hope	hoping	hoped

But when they are added to words not ending in silent *-e* we get these spellings:

can	canning	canned
din	dinning	dinned
hop	hopping	hopped

These regular spelling changes also tell us how the preceding vowels are to be pronounced.

4. Standard English

In our society considerable value is often placed upon using the "right" kind of English. This, practically speaking, means standard English—the vocabulary, pronunciation, and grammatical forms used by the educated people in the majority culture. Standard English is a class dialect and its mastery means that one has achieved a certain level of education, that he belongs to the majority group. It opens doors to social and economic opportunity which might be closed otherwise, no matter how well-qualified one might be in other respects. Blacks and other minority members may find, for instance, that among all things which discriminate against them, their language is by no means the least. Often those who belong to a minority group in society speak a nonstandard dialect rather than the standard dialect of the majority group. It is a snobbish idea, of course, and to be regretted, that acceptance or rejection for a job or membership in any social group depends so much upon language habits, rather than upon intrinsic abilities and worth as a human being. But until society changes, we are stuck with the situation, and it remains a social reality that such a minor thing as saying *it don't* and *I seen* instead of *it doesn't* and *I saw* can keep a man from getting where he wants to go.

What is standard English specifically? It cannot easily be sorted out item for item. For one thing, it is not written down in any authoritarian volume that "this is standard English absolutely; this is not." Some dictionaries make attempts at labeling words as "standard" or "nonstandard," but they do not always agree with one another. And their main concern anyway is to talk about all words in use, not just those in good favor. There are handbooks of usage also, but they are not complete, dealing primarily with borderline questions.

It wouldn't do much good, anyway, to have such an authority because standard usage is always slowly changing. What is considered standard at any given time depends upon the current custom. As an extreme example, certain verb forms once ended with the suffix *-eth* (He leadeth), but that was long ago and custom has changed. As a more current example, it seems to be no longer a capital crime to use *like* as a conjunction ("like a cigarette should") at least informally. It didn't used to be acceptable at all to purists, who did not take into account that *like* has been used as a conjunction by reputable writers for over four hundred years.

Variables in geography may also make a difference in deciding what is standard and what is not. To educated people in Southern Illinois the proper pronunciation of *greasy* is *greazy*, but to educated people in Northern Illinois the proper pronunciation is *greecey*. What is standard pronunciation in one section of the country may be nonstandard in another.

Standard English nevertheless has certain taboos which hold throughout the country: unconventional grammatical forms (Mike and me *clumb* the fence); unconventional vocabulary (This dude ripped me off); the double negative (I never did nothing); and shibboleth words (ain't, irregardless).

5. Usage

Usage is what standard English is all about, mainly. People confuse the term with *grammar*, as in "Oh, I had better watch my grammar, being as you're an English teacher." Grammar, however, is a description of the total way that a language operates; usage has to do with alternative choices in words and grammatical forms. In the past educated people have given lip service, at least, to the idea that any particular word or grammatical form had to be either correct or incorrect—absolutely right or absolutely wrong in all situations. Of late there has been a less simplistic view, chiefly because the studies of language specialists have convinced us of what we secretly believed all along: the actual ways in which we use language do not fit the neat "correct" or "incorrect" theory. It may have been suggested in the past by schoolmarms that the best speaker of English was one who sounded like a "walking dictionary" at all times, but we certainly didn't want to sound like one, and we didn't. We now believe that the use of a word may be all right in one context but not necessarily in all contexts. It depends upon a variety of conditions pertaining to the speaker, his audience, and the language situation. Usage, then, is a matter of choices. One considers the available language options and makes the choice that suits conditions best.

In a broad theoretical sense, one can say that the "right" words are those that satisfy both the speaker and his audience, and they may vary with conditions, as already noted. Two major factors help determine the appropriateness of usage:

1. *The language of the group.* Another way of saying this might be: the language of the people one feels comfortable with or one works with. There are many groups in society, and they may differ—some subtly, some obviously—in vocabulary, pronunciation, grammatical usage, and general style. And 'they may differ for a variety of reasons: because of educational background, socio-economic background, sex, regional geography, age factors, occupations, and special interests. The talk after the game in the Los Angeles Rams' dressing room, for instance, is not at all like the conversation at a symphony tea. Each kind of conversation, however, is appropriate to the respective group and usually satisfying to its users. Since language is an essential part of all group activity, one had better speak the language of his group if he is to belong. Not that any warning is necessary—the need for language adjustment is always obvious.

It is not only possible to belong to more than one group at the same time but also to adjust one's language accordingly. We may use one kind of language on the job, another on the tennis court, another at home, and so on. To use a TV analogy, we have more than one language channel available and can switch from one to another as the need arises. Sometimes a channel switch is advantageous but not easily come by. A black inner-city youngster, for instance, might find that the standard English of the white culture is a distinct disadvantage to him on his home ground, since it marks him as an outsider and perhaps not to be trusted. For him the pronunciation, the grammar, and the vocabulary of his own culture is right in that setting. But in a different setting, in the white culture where standard English is the group dialect, the reverse would be true. In a situation like this where one must try to be at home in two worlds, the best language response might be to switch channels from one dialect to another as the occasion requires.

Vocabulary is the obvious differential in group language. Boys, for instance, don't use words like *darling* and *sweet* to describe the sweater their friend is wearing, as girls might. Nor do they usually talk about colors in the same way that girls do: to most boys *magenta* is just plain red or purplish red; *coral* is pink, and so on.

Likewise, a typical speaker in his teens and twenties may often be identified because his speech includes much current slang. Expressions like *far out, getting my head on straight, cool, tough, rip off, heavy time, bad vibes,* and *putting it all together* would currently suggest that the speaker is under thirty and a bit on the hip side—especially when such slang is used profusely. Older people use slang also—everybody does—but they are not likely to use as much of it, and it is likely to be of a mixed vintage, including some current expressions and some hangovers from earlier days that have fallen out of use among younger speakers.

Any special interest group will have a body of "inside" words and expressions which are useful to them. Many examples can be cited: golf with its *par, birdie, eagle, slice,* and *hook;* tennis with its *lob, forehand, service, love, let ball,* and *fault;* and surfing with its *foam paipos, being stoked, getting in the tube, doing 360's,* and *jamming.*

One particular kind of vocabulary is called *shoptalk,* which is the lingo of occupations. For example, in the field of building construction a *sleeper* is not a late riser; a *riser* is not someone who gets up in the morning; a *water table* is not a spinoff from the water bed; a *rabbet* doesn't have long ears; *coping* is not handling life's problems as they come along; and a *cant strip* is not a reluctant showgirl. They, of course, are special terms used in carpentry. It is easy to have fun with shoptalk, but one should not forget that it serves a useful purpose. It enables a worker to communicate accurately with another worker about what he is doing. Furthermore, it is a sign that he knows his business. An apprentice carpenter who says that something is *level* when he means *plumb* is revealing his lack of carpentry knowledge and experience.

2. *The formality range.*   Besides adjusting usage to the standards of the group, most people also adjust it instinctively to the degrees of formality or informality of the total language situation. A familiar analogy is to compare our language to our clothes in this

respect: for formal occasions we dress up; for informal occasions we dress down, suiting our dress to the situation. The analogy is still valid, but in an age which seems to be rejecting formalism, our ideas of what is appropriate for formal occasions are beginning to change (mostly because of the influence of the youth movements). Although we still recognize a formal situation, we treat it with more freedom than formerly, both in our dress and in our language. Much serious writing is cast in informal English these days, rather than in the stricter usage of formal English. Formal English is now chiefly reserved for public events and writings of high intent: religious and ceremonial rites, speeches by important personages, and legal and other documents designed to be impressive. It may partake of literary words, which are fancier than conversational English; it may include archaic or legalistic expressions like *dost, thee, albeit,* and *bequeath;* but it will admit of no slang or contractions. Its grammar is traditional, its sentences long, and its cadences rhythmic. A familiar sample of formal English follows:

> We hold these truths to be self-evident, that all men are created equal; that they are endowed by their Creator with certain inalienable rights; that among these are life, liberty, and the pu it of happiness. That to secure these rights, governments are instituted among men, deriving their just powers from the consent of the governed; that, whenever any form of government becomes destructive of these ends, it is the right of the people to alter or abolish it, and to institute new government, laying its foundation on such principles, and organizing its powers in such form, as to them shall seem most likely to effect their safety and happiness.

> —*The Declaration of Independence*

Informal written English, which carries the burden of most printed matter these days (books, magazines, and newspapers), may be less impressive in tone than formal English, but it moves faster, is perhaps more readable, and is appropriate for almost all occasions. Since it is designed rather more to inform than to impress, its sentences are shorter and less ponderous than those of formal English. Ideally, its vocabulary is well-chosen, precise, but not stilted. Its vocabulary base is broader than that of formal English and draws from all levels of language—including the slang expression when the occasion really justifies it. Informal written English still adheres to the conventions of grammar as set forth by publishers' and editors' style books—distinctions between the uses of *lie* and *lay*, *he* and *him*, *like* and *as* are still observed, for instance—but it still reflects the more liberal present usage, rather than that of the past.

By way of illustration, the excerpt from the Declaration of Independence might look like this in informal written English:

> Everyone knows that these things are true: God made everyone equal and gave them the right to live, to be free, and to try to be happy. To make sure of these rights, men have set up governments which get their power from the people themselves. If a government doesn't use that power fairly, then the people have the right to change or do away with it and establish a new government that will give them the chance to be safe and happy.

Informal spoken English is generally more relaxed than written English, and for an obvious reason: speech generally occurs spontaneously and the speaker lacks time to make thoughtful, deliberate choices in vocabulary, grammar, and sentence structure. His revisions, for example, have to occur during the act of speaking, not later and at his leisure. Since speaking is not a prepared-for situation, as is writing, less is expected of the speaker in matters of formality. The following distinctions may be evident to one degree or another in informal speech, depending upon the verbal skill and sophistication of the speaker:

The make-do word: "Yesterday we took a job interest *test*. . . . (inventory)

The revision of thought: "Yesterday we took a job interest test . . . I mean it was an inventory, not really a test. . . ."

Slang expressions: "The reporters kept *hassling* him about what had gone on at the conference. . . ."

Relaxed usage: "*Like* I said, that's no way to make friends. . . ."

It should be noted that these are only general characteristics. Some few people have no relaxed speech and talk exactly as they write. Some abhor the slang term; others would no more confuse the case of *who* and *whom* than they would sit down to dinner and eat spaghetti with their fingers. But we are speaking here of the trend, not the exceptions.

Casual English has been called "language with its shoes off." It is used between close friends and family members—people who know each other so well that they need not keep up a language "front," as is necessary with outsiders. It may include the special family expressions which develop over a long time in such relationships, like the word *hangabur,* originally a child's mispronunciation of *hamburger,* but now humorously part of the family dialect. Or like the names for the old family dog—"Lassie" to outsiders, but "Boo Boo," "Digger," or "Meathead" to insiders. Not that normal usage and vocabulary disappear in casual English, but there are subtle variations. Since the users share the same background information on most topics, less information is needed when they communicate. ("Seen ol' whatzisname?" "Not since the bustup.") Statements may be fragmentary; thoughts may be left unfinished; words may be omitted; and grammar and vocabulary may be unconventional. Sometimes a grunt can do the job of a whole sentence in other circumstances. On the scale of formality, casual English is, of course, the most informal.

6. Vocabularies: Care and Feeding of

Since a vocabulary comes from "doing what comes naturally"—speaking, reading, listening, writing—it doesn't require any special effort just to have one. It begins when one learns to listen and speak at his mother's knee and continues to grow as one gets older. Naturally, some people have larger vocabularies than others. The reasons are various:

1. *Being smart.* Intelligence is something people are born with. Intelligent people are more likely to deal with words and to accumulate more of them than those who are less intelligent. Psychologists argue whether or not an IQ (Intelligence Quotient) can be increased, but it is certainly true that basic intelligence can be more fully realized through the acquisition of words. Nobody knows for sure just how close the relationship is between

words and the whole process of thinking; it may be that a limited vocabulary limits thinking as well.

2. *Being in a verbal environment.*   It helps to be around people who have a good command of language because it rubs off. In some homes, for example, families talk a lot among themselves about many things, and words are familiar and valuable commodities. Parents who promote good conversation at the dinner table and elsewhere with their children are making a contribution to vocabulary development. The same applies to those families who keep good magazines, newspapers, and books around the house. One can also deliberately try to broaden his verbal environment, that is, cultivate people and experiences that will challenge his vocabulary. It is a truism in a sport like tennis, for instance, that nobody improves his game by playing against someone poorer or just as good as he is. The real improvement comes when he plays against someone better. The same applies to wordplay.

3. *Doing different things.*   Since every human activity is associated with language, each new experience can mean new words to go along with it, whether it be gardening, a photography class, learning a different job skill, traveling to Europe (or maybe just out of the neighborhood), learning to drive, playing chess, getting involved in political or community movements, or building a house. Experience builds vocabulary at first hand.

4. *Getting educated.*   Grade school, high school, and college are "word factories" where words are met in a structured setting, that is, in discussions, lectures, textbooks, tapes, and records. The higher the level of education, the greater the word exposure and the more words that are likely to enter the vocabulary. Now that adult education classes have become an important part of our culture, the vocabulary growth that comes with formal education can continue throughout one's life if so desired.

5. *Reading a lot.*   The best way to meet most uncommon words is in print. The person who reads because he likes to read is continually enlarging his recognition vocabulary by meeting all kinds of words over and over in different contexts. With enough contexts, essential meanings come through, even for the most

abstruse words. Over a long period of time a steady reader will inevitably acquire a large vocabulary. Reading habitually can really accelerate word learning, since the more one reads the better a reader he becomes, and the better the reader he becomes, the more he is likely to read and to understand. It is a beneficial circle.

7. Getting Interested in Words

Much has been written about guaranteed ways to achieve a better vocabulary. In fact, on drugstore and supermarket racks can be found dozens of books which seem to promise a new vocabulary in almost no time. Their contents expose the reader to any number of hard words, and presumably he could memorize them through looking up their definitions and doing follow-up exercises. But one of the troubles with this method is that the reader is arbitrarily introduced to words which are of primary interest to the author; he does not meet them in any natural context of his own interest or experience. Thirty days after having started (and presumably finished) a book, he will have forgotten many of the words simply because they were not sufficiently meaningful when presented. As a result he will have added only a comparatively few words to his basic vocabulary. To achieve real word growth, he would have to continue working in such books the rest of his life, and if that is the only word exercise he indulged in, it is doubtful that such growth would come.

The only realistic way to a better vocabulary is the hard way: to cultivate a close and prolonged involvement with words throughout one's life. Also—and this is important—in order to learn more words and meanings it is helpful to know something about words as a phenomenon of language—their origins, the ways in which meanings develop and spread and change, their forms, their spellings and pronunciations, their idiosyncrasies, the ways in which they influence human behavior, their usage, and so forth. In short, to know all about them. When one is interested in racing or baseball he soon knows the names and characteristics of cars, drivers, or players. He doesn't have to sit down and memorize lists of them; they come to him because he is interested in the subject. When one becomes involved closely with words, the same thing happens.

He soon knows many, many words because he is interested in them. Hopefully, this book—with its focus on words and on our great word repository, the dictionary—will help the reader achieve that goal.

Exercises

1. How completely are you dependent upon language? Keep a log for a specified period—an hour, a morning, a day— and record each time words are a part of your consciousness. Count all language activities—speaking, reading, listening, and writing. Share results with the class.

2. New words and new meanings for old words are coined every year. For example, these have recently appeared in print and may or may not be still current when you read this in print: *ecofreak, cold rodder, urbicidal, workaholic, hot pants, condomarinium*, and *job bank*. With the exception of *cold rodder* (a snowmobile enthusiast), meanings of these words can be easily inferred by anyone who has a good word sense. Discuss possible definitions for each of these and explain how they were arrived at. What other new words can you add to the list?

3. As pointed out already in this chapter, the sounds of words in actual speech may be different from the sounds of those same words pronounced in isolation. Test this statement by monitoring the informal speech of a friend, teacher, or family member and making brief notes on stream-of-speech pronunciation. Have a few examples ready for class analysis and discussion.

4. It is quite possible for a word to have more than one acceptable pronunciation, since language is a human activity subject to many variables. What is your own normal pronunciation for each of the words below? What other pronunciations does the dictionary list?

rodeo	Oregon	gibber	creek
crayfish	Illinois	harass	chimpanzee
catsup	route	coupon	caramel
automobile	Vietnam	Hawaii	motorcycle

5. Can one think without using words? Some people maintain that it is impossible to do this, that even silent thought needs words to

work with. Others claim that they can think without words by visualizing objects, scenes, pictures of what they are thinking about. What do you think? Define "thinking."

6. Each new baby has the ability to make certain gurgles, cries, goos, and other sounds at birth, or very soon after, but is incapable of speech or language. Yet by the time the child is five or six years old, it has mastered most of the grammar of a language system—whether it be English, Chinese, Arabic, or Swahili. How much is language ability a biological gift a child is born with? How much of it is learned behavior? The language shelf in the library should supply ample material for this and the following question.

7. No one knows how spoken language ever got started, but scholars have advanced interesting hypotheses from time to time—for example, the "ding-dong" theory, the "bow-wow" theory, and the "pooh-pooh" theory. Read up on these and any other more recent ones you find and be ready to discuss them in class.

8. Has the case for standard English been overstated? Are new social forces diminishing its importance? Richard W. Hall in his article, "A Muddle of Models: The Radicalizing of American English" (*English Journal, May* 1972), suggests that the rising militancy and power of minority groups and the growing rejection by the younger generation of traditional upper and middle class values are making for many speech standards rather than one. What evidence can you offer that bears on this statement?

9. Start your career as a wordwatcher. Carry a small notebook around and keep a record of words which interest you. They may be words new to you, words used cleverly, words with interesting meanings or different pronunciations, words you'd like to use yourself sometime, and so on. From time to time spend a class period sharing notebooks.

Bibliography

The following books were useful in compiling the information in this chapter. They are also recommended to the student who wishes further reading.

Fries, Charles C. *Linguistics and Reading*. New York: Holt, Rinehart and Winston, Inc.

Hill, Archibald, ed. *Linguistics Today*. New York: Basic Books Inc., 1969.

Hudspeth, Robert N., and Donald F. Sturtevant, eds. *The World of Language—A Reader in Linguistics*. New York: American Book Company, 1967.

Laird, Charlton. "Language and the Dictionary," *Webster's New World Dictionary of the American Language*, second edition. New York: The World Publishing Company, 1970.

O'Neil, Wayne, "The Spelling and Pronunciation of English," *The American Heritage Dictionary of the English Language*. Boston: American Heritage Publishing Company, Inc., 1969.

Shuy, Roger W. *Discovering American Dialects*. Champaign, Illinois: National Council of Teachers of English, 1967.

2

Words and History

1. Borrowing

In its early beginnings, English (or *Englisc,* as it was written then) had a comparatively "pure" vocabulary. That is, it contained few words taken from other languages. When a new word was needed, it was created either by adding a prefix or suffix to a native word or by compounding—putting two or more old words together to form a new one. For instance, after Christianity was reintroduced into England, the word *gospel* was created out of two older words, *god* and *spell*—literally, "good tale."

The vocabulary has changed considerably since those early times. Instead of being composed of native words almost exclusively, it now contains words from many other languages. Language specialists tell us that well over one half of the words in our dictionary have been borrowed at one time or another from other sources, principally from Latin, Greek, and French. Clearly, word borrowing has been an important means of adding to our vocabulary.

If English had been left to develop in isolation, it would have borrowed fewer words. But English not only rubbed elbows with other languages, it collided head-on with one or two. When things happen to a people—conquest, trade, exploration, cultural explosions—things happen to their language as well. Most noticeably, the vocabulary is enriched as the people encounter new customs, inventions, and ideas. Thus, in a sense, each one of the words which were borrowed into English is a small part of English history, and a discussion of word borrowing leads inevitably to the history of the English-speaking peoples.

In this chapter we will focus on the important events which helped to shape our vocabulary. A good starting point will be the language family from which English claims descent.

2. The Indo-European Family of Languages

Several thousand different languages are spoken in the world today. These are the individual members of perhaps a dozen language families whose roots go far back into man's early days before recorded history. One of these families, *Indo-European*, is of special interest to us. Half the population of the earth speak languages which are members of this family, and, more important perhaps, it is the family to which our own language belongs. It is generally agreed that Indo-European, this parent language of English, must have been generated in the Near East and spoken as far north as north-central Europe as long as 5,000 years ago. No one knows exactly where it originated, or what the people were like who spoke it, nor has anyone ever seen any written examples of it. Nevertheless, the philologists who study language history are sure that the majority of modern European languages and a number of important Asiatic languages are offspring of this single ancient tongue. Perceiving that certain basic words in a number of languages are very similar to each other and wanting to know why, these philologists painstakingly compared the vocabulary and grammar of each language. They found that the likenesses were family resemblances, evidence that these modern languages were born as dialects of a single language along ago. When these dialects spread for various reasons over Europe and parts of India, they developed as time went on into separate languages.

Language scientists have reconstructed the basic elements of Indo-European and can trace many modern words back to these I.E. roots. For example, *cat* goes ultimately back to the I.E. base *qat-*, meaning "to bear young." It is interesting to contemplate how a few thousand Indo-European roots have given birth to countless words in many languages.

Here are the main branches of the Indo-European family:

1. Hittite, a now-dead language which was spoken in the area occupied by modern Turkey.

2. Tokharian, another dead language, which used to flourish in the area of Chinese Turkestan. Both Hittite and Tokharian have left no living language descendants.

3. Indo-Iranian, which includes Persian, the languages of India, and classical Sanskrit.

4. Hellenic, which includes ancient and modern Greek.

5. Armenian, which is spoken in part of what is now Russian territory.

6. Italic, which includes ancient Latin and its derivatives—Italian, French, Spanish, Portuguese, Rumanian, and several minor languages. All these are called *Romance* languages because they came from the Latin, or Roman, parent.

7. Celtic, which includes Welsh and Gaelic. Gaelic is spoken in parts of Scotland, and an attempt has been made to revive its use in part of Ireland.

8. Balto-Slovak, which includes Polish, Czechoslovakian, Russian, and Bulgarian.

9. Albanian, which is spoken in Albania and in a small part of Italy.

10. Germanic, which in ancient times had three main branches which have developed in this fashion—

Eastern	*Northern*	*Western*
Gothic (dead)	*(From Old Norse:)*	*(From High German:)*
	Swedish	modern German
	Norwegian	*(From Low German:)*
	Danish	Dutch
	Icelandic	Frisian
		Plattdeutsch
		English

Modern English, then, came from the Germanic branch of the Indo-European family, and its cousin languages include, among others, French, Italian, Latin, Greek, Russian, and even classical Indian Sanskrit.

Naturally, English did not first appear upon the stage of history just as we know it today. It passed through two earlier phases which we call the period of *Middle English* (1100–1500) and the period of *Old English* (450–1100). The Old English period is also called the Anglo-Saxon period, after the tribes who brought our early language to Britain.

3.   The Period of Old English (450–1100)

Even before the English language was spoken there, the island of Britain had an interesting history. The first Britons of whom we have any real record were a primitive people called the Celts. They spoke a language which was an ancestor of modern Welsh and the Gaelic of Ireland and Scotland. In 55 B.C. Julius Caesar led the first Roman invasion of the island. He and later Roman invaders finally subjugated most of the Celts. Rome occupied Britain militarily for roughly 400 years, imposing Roman law and order and leaving its mark upon the landscape with five superb highways, Roman baths complete with heating equipment and piped water supplies, and houses built in the Roman style. Even today, farmers occasionally turn up with their plows relics dating back to the Roman occupation—an old Roman coin, a metal drinking vessel, or perhaps a cooking pot.

The Roman occupation came to an end in A.D. 409–410, when Rome began to have such great trouble on the Continent with barbarian invasions that she called her legions home to fight. They left little of their Latin language behind—at least, few words of Latin from this period have entered English. One Roman word which did show up later in the names of towns is the Latin word for *camp, castra.* It is found in names such as *Winchester, Chester,* and *Lancaster.* A few of the old Celtic place names found a home in the language as well—*Kent, Thames, Avon,* and possibly *London,* to name several we have all heard of.

With the Romans gone, the Celts had only a short breathing space. Three Germanic tribes—the Jutes, the Angles, and the Saxons—began to press across the Channel starting about A.D. 450. During the next two centuries the Celts were driven into the mountains of Wales and Scotland. The invaders, fierce and roving tribesmen similar in appearance and custom to the Vikings of later history, were the founders of the English nation and speakers of the language which we call *native English.* This Old English, or Anglo-Saxon, is difficult for us to read today. Yet many words, taken individually, are recognizable if you make allowances for spelling and pronunciation differences: *fæder (father), eorl (earl), sittan* (*to sit*), *hring* (*ring*), *hund* (*hound*), and *hūs* (*house*), for example.

How did the first English-speaking tribes fare in this land taken from the Celts? The Angles, the Saxons, and the Jutes each settled in different parts of England. Although they fought among themselves, they were very similar in language and culture, and eventually fused into one people, speaking different dialects. They ruled separately at first in strongholds, then in small kingdoms, and finally merged into one nation under Kings Egbert and Alfred in the ninth century. Their land was called by several names during its early history—*Saxonia, Anglia,* and *Englaland,* which means literally "land of the Angles."

The number of foreign words in the Old English vocabulary was small. Some Latin words had been acquired from traders in Europe even before the migration to England—*wine, cheap* (meaning "to bargain" at first), *kettle, cup,* and the like. Others were brought into England through the church as missionaries converted the Anglo-Saxons to Christianity. Words such as *monk, priest, abbot, angel, noon, nun, organ, shrine, meter,* and *fever* are examples.

Another kind of language interchange started just before the beginning of the ninth century, when the Scandinavians, or Danes, cast covetous eyes on England and began to move in on their English cousins. Before the end of the century they had migrated in such numbers and had fought so fiercely that in the Peace of Wedmore, A.D. 878, the English were forced to settle half of England on these Vikings. The Danes agreed to remain in their part of the territory, to be known thereafter as the *Danelaw* ("land under Danish law"), and to accept Christianity. The language and culture of the Danes was similar to that of the English—they had the same words for such basics as *man, wife, father, house, sorrow, winter, summer, think, see,* and *wise*—and they could understand each other without much difficulty.

Still, not all words were alike. As time went on, Danish words began to appear in English. Some replaced English words; others were used as synonyms. Most noticeable additions from the Danish are words containing the *sk* sound, words such as *skull, skulk, sky, scant, skill, skin, scrape, bask,* and *skirt.*

The *sk* sound paralleled the *sh* sound in English in some words. Thus we got the word *shirt* from Anglo-Saxon and *skirt* from the Danish; both meant much the same thing at first. English also received three personal pronouns from Danish: *they, their,* and *them,* which replaced the native forms. Like the Celts, the Danes left their words on the landscape of England. Their endings *by,* meaning "town," and *thorp,* meaning "village," are reflected in the last part of names like *Derby, Rugby,* and *Dunthorpe.*

Although fighting between the Danes and Anglo-Saxons continued intermittently, by the year 1000 language distinctions between the two had begun to fade. The separate vocabularies were mixing, and, since they were so much alike in important respects anyway, they could be considered as one. English continued to be the basic language, but it was enriched by almost 1,000 Danish words.

Exercises

1. Here is an Old English version of the Lord's Prayer,[1] followed by an early modern English version. After you have read them both, copy the Old English version on a sheet of paper and try to fill in above or below each line a literal translation for each word. Be sure that you leave space between the lines for writing the words in. After you have done this you will be ready for the questions which will follow. Note: the marks þ and ð represent the *th* sound.

Fæder ūre,
þū þe eart on heofonum,
Sī þīn nama gehālgod.
Tobecume þīn rīce.
Gewurþe ðīn willa on eorðan swā swā on heofonum.   5
Ūrne gedaeghwāmlīcan hlāf syle ūs tō dæg.
And forgyf ūs ūre gyltas, swā swā wē forgyfað ūrum gyltendum.
And ne gelæd þū ūs on costnunge,
Ac ālys us of yfele. Sōþlīce.

Our Father which art in heaven,
Hallowed be thy name.
Thy kingdom come.
Thy will be done in earth as it is in heaven.
Give us this day our daily bread.   5
And forgive us our debts, as we forgive our debtors.
And lead us not into temptation,
But deliver us from evil.   Amen.

---

[1] Baugh, Albert C. *A History of the English Language,* second edition. New York: Appleton-Century-Crofts. Inc., 1957.

a. List all the words from the Old English version which you think have disappeared from the language.

b. List all the words which are still in the language, even though changed in some way.

c. Point out any differences in sentence word order from early English to Old English.

d. A German word for *government* or *kingdom* is *reich*. Can you find any word resembling it in the Old English version?

e. Can you find the following words in the Old English version: *sooth* (*truth*), *guilts, loaf, day* (note that *aeg* changes to *ey ey* or *ay* in Middle English)?

f. Old English was an inflected language; that is, certain words changed form depending upon their function in a sentence— direct object, subject, indirect object, possessive, and so on. Can you list any words in the Old English version which change form and appear with various spellings?

g. Can you think of any modern English words which change their form, depending upon their grammatical use in a sentence?

2. Here is the word *mother* as it occurs in various Indo-European languages:

Swedish: moder	Danish: mor
German: Mutter	Dutch: moeder
Spanish: madre	French: mére
Italian: madre	Portuguese: mãe

By consulting foreign language dictionaries or by asking people you know who speak a foreign language, try to find the foreign equivalents for these basic English words: *yes, no, three, father, ten, I, house.* Discuss their similarities to the English words and their differences.

3. Discuss: If you were a language specialist making comparative language studies, what kinds of words would you compare for language similarities? What similarities besides those of vocabulary would you look for?

SPECIAL PROJE

1. For research and report, investigate any one of these topics— the story of Beowulf, the Anglo-Saxon epic hero; characteristics of Anglo-Saxon poetry; the development of the English alphabet; the

Greek alphabet; the Russian alphabet. Consult the literature and language shelves of your library for resource material.

2. Secure a copy of the newspaper *The Christian Science Monitor*, which carries on its editorial page each day a religious message translated into a foreign language. Scan the translation for words which are recognizably close in appearance to English words. Make a list of the words and discuss them in class.

3. From the *Monitor* collect a number of foreign language translations—a different language is used each day—and make a bulletin board display.

4. Tristan de Cunha is a group of three volcanic islands in the South Atlantic belonging to Great Britain. The inhabitants of these small islands had lived there for generations, seldom having any contact with the rest of the world. Several years ago the British found it necessary to evacuate the islands and transfer the people to Britain. They immediately became of great importance to students of language, for the people were found to be speaking the English of the nineteenth century, the time of Queen Victoria and Charles Dickens. In effect, their language was essentially the English of over one hundred years ago!

Investigate this story to find out more about the islanders' language habits, the effect of isolation upon a language community, and what happens to a language when its speakers are suddenly exposed to a more modern linguistic environment. Check on these articles: "Annals of Migration," *The New Yorker*, November 9, 1963; "Back to Eden," *Newsweek*, April 1, 1963; "Far-off Exiles of Tristan," *Life*, July 12, 1963; and "Home to Lonely Tristan de Cunha," *The National Geographic Magazine*, June 1964.

4. The Period of Middle English (1100–1500)

The next impact upon the language was the greatest it was ever to receive—the conquest of England by the Norman French. The conquest marked the end of the Old English period and the beginning of the Middle English period. This time the conquerors came from Normandy, a province of France on the coast across the English Channel from England. The ancestors of these Normans had been vikings, who like their cousins the Danes had gone looking for richer homelands. They conquered and settled Normandy in the eighth and ninth centuries and very quickly adopted the language and culture of the French who were living there. The name *Normandy* came from the name by which the invaders were known—*Norsemen*. By 1066 the Normans had become thoroughly French, and their leader, William the Conqueror, was using the pretext of a distant blood relationship to lay claim to the vacant throne of England.

When Harold, a Saxon noble, was given the throne, William invaded England. In a pitched battle at Hastings, William defeated Harold's army.

Within a year the Normans ruled all of England. The seat of government for the French court was London. As you can imagine, being a Saxon nobleman during this period was not the quickest way to fame and fortune. Many of the Saxon nobility were killed. Others were removed from their holdings, and their property and positions were given to Norman barons eager to cut up England as their own private pie. Norman French was decreed to be the language of the land, and soon all important business was transacted in French. It was taught in the schools, and it became the official language of the law courts and of government. Written English went underground for almost 200 years. Most literature written in England during this time was written in French or Latin.

With all these strikes against it, you might wonder how English managed to survive. Fortunately, the Normans' language controls did not reach down to the lower classes—the people who, in the long run, were to determine the fate of the language. It may be that the Normans did not have proper means to ensure that everyone learned and spoke French. More likely, they may not have cared what language the "unimportant" people spoke, since England was in the nature of a colonial possession, not necessarily a new homeland. In any case, the Normans left the lower classes alone. They were not pressured out of England, nor were they forced to learn French. So it happened that while French was the official language of England, English remained the actual language of most of its people.

Another reason that we speak English today instead of French is that the Norman rulers eventually lost their ties to France. They were unable through the years which followed to hold on to their continental lands and power, and they became Englishmen whether they liked it or not. Although they were bilingual—at home in both languages—English eventually became their primary dialect and French was a foreign language, still taught in schools, but not spoken as a native of Paris would speak it.

As old grudges faded with time and as the process of assimilation went its inevitable way, English began to reassert itself in the schools, the law courts, and in business. Although French and Latin were still considered to be the superior languages, even by the rest of Europe, many English writers were beginning to write good literature in their native language. Chaucer's *The Canterbury Tales*, written about 1400 in the London dialect, made it clear that the English language had come back into its own. It showed that a talented writer could create literature in English to compare with, and even exceed, anything written in French.

But the English of 1400 was not the English of 1066. It had changed, partly as a result of natural processes, partly as a direct result of the conquest and occupation. Its word order and grammar, as a result of natural change, more closely resembled that of modern English. In Old English a writer could place words in various positions in a sentence without affecting the meaning; internal changes in the forms of words and endings tacked onto words, like the *-um* in *heofonum*, *-a* in *nama*, *-as* in *gyltas*, and *-um* in *gyltendum* (as found in the Old English version of the Lord's Prayer), told the reader how the words functioned in a sentence. By the Middle English period these *inflections*, as they are called, were disappearing, and part of their job was being done by prepositions and by the arrangement of words within the sentence. You did not need a special ending on a word to know that it was a subject or an object of a verb. Its position within the sentence told you. If a noun came before a verb it was likely to be the subject; if it came after the verb, it was likely to be the object. Modern English still holds to this subject-verb-object pattern, and to the several other sentence patterns which we have become used to.

With a little vocabulary help, we can read the following lines of Middle English poetry from the prologue to Chaucer's *Canterbury Tales* without difficulty. It looks much less like a foreign language than does Old English.

Upon his arm he baar a gay bracer,°   (arm guard)
And by his syde a swerd and a bokeler,°   (shield)
And on that oother syde a gay daggere
Harneised° wel and sharp as point of spere   (mounted)

The vocabulary changes were as drastic as those in grammar. Many English words disappeared altogether, to be replaced by French words. For example, in the lines just quoted, six words— *gay, bracer, buckler, dagger, harnessed,* and *point*—came into English during the centuries after the Conquest. And this is but a sample taken at random.

French words were not adopted immediately after the invasion. It was a gradual process, but after 1250 they began showing up in numbers in the literature of the period. As you might expect, many words were borrowed from warfare. *Army, captain, lieutenant, sergeant, soldier, spy, vanquish, siege, banner, danger,* and, thankfully, *peace* remind us vividly that the French were conquerors.

And even in those days the French must have been interested in fine foods and cookery. They gave us the words *dinner* and *supper* (*breakfast* is English) and the word *cuisine,* as well as *sausage, toast, jelly, soup, roast,* and *pastry.* Sir Walter Scott pointed out in *Ivanhoe* that live animals (which were tended by the English peasants) had English names: *ox, cow, calf, sheep, swine, deer.* But when they appeared on the table and were eaten by the Norman masters, they had French names: *beef, veal, mutton, pork, bacon,* and *venison.*

So it went in every phase of life touched by French culture. Law, government, the church, fashion, house furnishings, the court, games and recreations, hunting and riding, medicine, art, and architecture were all represented by new words from the French. Some were synonyms for previous English words but many more were new, introducing ideas, things, and customs unfamiliar to the English. Years after the Conquest was all but forgotten, borrowing continued, although the center of influence had shifted from Normandy to Paris.

Altogether, thousands of words from the French found their way into English in the years between the eleventh and sixteenth centuries. Through hundreds of years of enforced and intimate contact with the French, both the culture and language of Britain were altered.

Exercises

1. The following poetry, written in the London dialect of about
1400, is again taken from the prologue of Geoffrey Chaucer's *Canterbury Tales*. Read it carefully, write out a translation of the lines into
modern English, so much as you understand them, and then answer
the questions which follow. (The lines describe a young squire of
the late Middle Ages.)

> Embrouded° was he as it were a meede,°   (embroidered; meadow)
> Al ful of fresshe floures white and redde.
> Syngynge he was or floytynge° al the day.   (fluting)
> He was as fressh as is the monthe of May.
> Short was his gowne with sleves longe and
>   wyde.
> Wel koude he sitte on hors and faire ryde.
> He koude songes make and wel endite,°   (compose words)
> Juste,° and eek daunce, and wel purtreye,° and   (joust; draw)
>   write.

How many words by actual count do you recognize as being current
in English today? Which words appear with the same spelling in
modern English? Which words have disappeared from the language?
2.   Take a sampling of the modern versions of any ten words from
this selection, look up their origins in the dictionary, and determine
how many of them came into the language after the Norman conquest. If a word appears with AS. or OE., the word was in use in
the Old English period. But if the word is designated as OF. (Old
French), MF. (Middle French), or ME. (Middle English), and AS.
or OE. does not appear there, it probably came into the language
during the Middle English period. This exercise should give you a
rough idea of how our vocabulary increased during this time. Compare your results with those of others in the class.
3.   Think of five words which relate specifically to one of these
areas—religion, law, or government (like *judge, writ, lawyer*, for
example). Write them down; then look up the etymology of each
in the dictionary. If we are correct in our assumption that many
words in these areas came from the French during the Middle English period, the dictionary should indicate it. Even if no more than
three out of five of your words are so designated, this is a significant
number. Write a short paragraph summarizing your findings.

5. The Period of Modern English (After 1500)

The next great inflow of words came into English from Latin and Greek in the period of Modern English. By the time of Shakespeare in the sixteenth century, English had changed in vocabulary, pronunciation, and grammar to such a degree that the language of Chaucer was archaic. Vowel sounds and syllable stresses had altered noticeably and inflectional endings continued to disappear. The vocabulary had increased tremendously, chiefly because of the Renaissance, an intellectual and cultural movement which swept over Europe and England beginning in the late Middle Ages and continuing into the seventeenth century. The Renaissance started as educated men rediscovered the world of classical Greece and Rome, which had been partly forgotten during the Middle Ages. It began as a love affair with anything classical: art, philosophy, history, government, literature, and whatever else was ancient. After a time it expanded into a pursuit of modern knowledge as well. Its results were discoveries in science, medicine, and general learning, inventions like the printing press, and the creation of masterworks of art and literature in the Western European countries.

A major by-product of this cultural rebirth was a belief among many English writers and scholars that what English needed was a large dose of Latin and Greek words. Were not these the languages in which the great writers of ancient times had achieved near perfection? If English were ever to reach such heights, it must imitate Greek and Latin. So went their reasoning. You have already encountered the hard word dictionaries in Chapter 1, and you may remember that many of the words in them were ridiculous. Some were used only once—when they were transferred from a Latin to an English dictionary by an enthusiastic lexicographer. Many Greek and Latin borrowings were more sensible, however, and won a place in the language through gradual use. There was a real need for words to keep pace with men's expanding knowledge.

A great many of the Latin and Greek words were borrowed in part, as prefixes (word beginnings), suffixes (word endings), and roots. Such derivations from Latin and Greek are now so common in English that many people mistakenly think that English must have descended straight from the classical languages. And it is true that these elements lend themselves conveniently to the formation of new words. For example, *auto*, a Greek form meaning "self," has given meaning to almost 300 words in modern English. Other useful borrowed affixes include *-ology*, as in *methodology; inter-*, as in *interscholastic; pre-*, as in *prelude;* and *pro-*, as in *pronoun.*

We have many words which are made up of combinations of borrowed parts, like *misanthrope* (*missein*, "to hate," plus *anthropos*, "a man") and *reiterate* (*re-*, "again," plus *iterare*, "to say again"). The *re-* prefix is a very handy one. It can be placed in front of almost any English verb to form a new word. Occasionally we combine both Latin and Greek elements to form one word, as in the scientific word *spectroscope*. The first half of the word is from the Latin; the last half is from the Greek.

As a rule, the words borrowed from these languages are the kind which are used formally rather than in everyday conversation, perhaps because they were pushed into the language mainly through writing. Here is a small sampling: *propagate* (L.), *anonymous* (Gr.), *agile* (L.), *emancipate* (L.), *admiration* (L.), *catastrophe* (Gr.), *interrogate* (L.), *misanthrope* (Gr.), *reiterate* (L.), *auxiliary* (L.), and *epitome* (Gr.). There are thousands more.

The borrowing from Greek and Latin is still going on, by the way. Physics, botany, biology, zoology, chemistry, geology—in fact, all areas of science—turn to Greek and Latin when new words are needed. *Penicillin, astrophysics*, and *sulfa* come immediately to mind as examples.

The Renaissance also gave us words directly from French, Spanish, and Italian. Many arrived as a result of exploration, for this period was also the age of English discovery, with men like Drake and Raleigh carrying the English flag to little known parts of the world. Some of these words like *cannibal, tobacco, potato*, and *banana*—had been used first by the Spanish, and were quickly absorbed into the vocabulary of the English, who traveled the same sea lanes.

Other words like *bank* (It. and Fr.), *balcony* (It.), *volcano* (Fr. and It.), and *algebra* (It. from Ar.) were borrowed as a result of commerce and English travel abroad. We know that young Englishmen of means must have gone to Italy in particular to be educated and to travel, since we read scolding references to "Italianate Englishmen" in literature of the late 1500's. These travelers brought back not only new words, but also, according to one contemporary critic, Roger Ascham, "plenty of new mischiefs never known in

England before." (A proverb in Shakespeare's time was "An Italianate Englishman is a devil incarnate!")

Following the Renaissance, English has continued to be a word-borrowing language, perhaps not at the same pace as during that period, but certainly at a fairly regular rate. From wherever English soldiers were sent for colonization, from wherever English and American ships docked for trade, from wherever jet airlines have carried English-speaking tourists and businessmen, words have been added to the English tongue. Borrowing into both British and American English continues from all continents.

From the American Indians came *tomahawk, wigwam, squaw, teepee, wampum,* and countless names on the land—*Willamette, Snohomish, Nebraska, Sioux City, Allegheny, Kentucky, Walla Walla, Seattle,* and *Dakota.*

From the Spanish in America came *mustang, ranch, patio, bonanza, rodeo, vigilante, sombrero, vamoose, hoosegow,* and, most recently, *bracero.* From India, through the period of British colonization, came *thug, loot, pajamas, bandana,* and *sahib.* From the Dutch came *easel, sketch, yacht, boss,* and *deck.* From the Germans came *kindergarten, semester, delicatessen, blitz* and *blitzkrieg, frankfurter, wiener,* and the universal *hamburger.* So much of the French has entered our language that a listing would be superfluous. It is interesting to note, however, that the borrowing is still continuing. The latest words from France are *discotheque* and *a go-go.*

English has borrowed more words and word parts than has any other language. The Anglo-Saxon vocabulary of about 50,000 words has increased to well over 600,000 words and the end is not in sight. Words are created by many means, as we shall see in the next chapter, but borrowing has accounted for our greatest language growth. It is one of the factors which have made ours a great language.

6. "Reverse English"

"Reverse English" is a slang term which a pool player might use to describe the backspin imparted to a cue ball. But let's twist the meaning for a moment to make an important point: English, which through the centuries has imported words in great numbers from other languages, has become such a force in the world that many of its words, in turn, have become popular exports. Our word *automobile* has been adopted without spelling change into French and Italian, and with minor changes into Spanish (*automovil*) and Swedish (*automobil*). And this is how two American institutions appear in other European languages:

Fr.	aspirine	base-ball
Sp.	aspirina	beisbol
G.	Aspirin	Baseball
It.	aspirina	giuoco a palla
Sw.	aspirin	baseball

Notice that only in the Italian expression for *baseball* has a word been converted to a native equivalent.

The popular culture of America and the sheer power of our world-wide influence have caused many words like these to be introduced overseas. If you were to read German newspapers, you would recognize English words such as *scoop, paperbacks, teenagers, holiday, blue jeans, cowboys* and *Indians, toasters,* and *mixers.* Sports terms such as *ref, goalkeeper, puck, body check, punch, boxing,* and *photofinish* would also be familiar.

Even the Russians are noting the arrival of English words into their language. Though the spelling is a bit different, the source is still evident in the housewife's *mikser* and *toster,* the airplane traveler's *stuardesa,* the car driver's *antifriz,* the engineer's *komputer,* and the worker's free *vikend.*

Not that the influx of such Americanisms is always welcomed abroad. A Spanish writer complained in a Madrid newspaper that "infusions of Anglo-Saxon words are making the Spanish language an English colony." He deplored the use of such non-Spanish words as *romance, motor,* and *gas.*

The French, who long ago formed the Académie Francais for the purpose of trying to keep the language pure, have started an "American English, Go Home!" movement. Officially known as the Committee for the Defense and Expansion of French, they are fighting against what they consider to be the corruption of their language by such words as *le drugstore, skyscraper, weekend, shopping, parking,* and *quick lunch,* all common usage in France. Obviously, many of the French must like the English words or find them convenient. Otherwise, the academicians would have nothing to be concerned about.

7. World Englishes

French purists are playing a losing game. Not only are English words infiltrating other cultures, but English itself has replaced French as the world's second language. Wherever he goes in the world, the American traveler can find someone who understands at least a few English words. In many countries English is taught side by side with the native tongues, beginning in the early grades.

English is not the language spoken by the greatest number of speakers; Chinese has that honor. According to world population figures published in the *United Nations Demographic Yearbook* in March 1970, the Chinese number over 730 million (and current unofficial estimates suggest that by now it is much closer to 800 million). The total number of English speakers in the world, both native and foreign, has been estimated at 700 million. One might argue that the differences between some Chinese dialects are so great that they really 'constitute separate languages—that the Chinese are not really speaking one language, but several. However, this point-of-view is not universally accepted. Nevertheless, it cannot be denied that English, because of its increasingly pervasive usage all over the globe, is the closest thing there is today to an international language.

British colonization and migration have accounted for much of the spread of English across the globe: New Zealand, Australia, South Africa, Canada, India, and the United States testify to this fact. Travel, trade, World War II, and succeeding military engagements such as those in Korea and Vietnam have also helped account for the spread of English. And since America has in this century replaced England as the major English-speaking power in the world, it is American English which has become increasingly prominent on foreign shores.

As you might suspect, many of the Englishes spoken around the world occasionally differ from one another in pronunciation, idiom, and vocabulary; yet speakers of English can readily understand almost any variety. One kind of English which we would not understand well at first is Pidgin-English, spoken by almost 50 million people. It is a trade language which developed in some of the Pacific islands and along the coast of southeastern Asia. Its structure and vocabulary vary with the locality, but it is essentially a compromise "make do" language, providing a way for people of different languages and cultures to communicate on a simple level. Pidgin-English is normally composed of four or five hundred English words combined with a few elements and words from the native language. The sentence patterns are basically English, but the grammatical forms of English are pretty much neglected. To our ears Pidgin is amusing, crude, and inadequate, but it has great utility, since it enables millions of people to communicate, even if only on a very basic level.

In Jamaica and Louisiana Pidgin-English evolved into creole languages, which are minglings of African slave languages with colonial British English and colonial French. In Australia Pidgin is the language bridge between the white settler and the bushman. You can hear it spoken at dockside in Korea, Vietnam, and Polynesia. In Indonesia, it is reported, a national language has been created, a combination of Malay and Pidgin-English. Here are a few of the more colorful Pidgin terms taken from several dialects over the world:

friend: Him brother belong me.

policeman: Gubmint catchum-fella.

moon: Lamp belong Jesus.

whiskers: Grass belong face.

piano: Big fellow bokus [box].

army chaplain: Missionary belong soldier.

the best: Numbah one.

the worst: Numbah ten. (G.I.'s in Vietnam have found this to be insufficient to describe their reactions to war conditions. They use "numbah ten thou"!)

In contrast with Pidgin-English, Australian, American, and British English appear to be one and the same language, as they are in all really important respects. What differences there are appear in interesting variations of pronunciation and vocabulary. Take Australian English for example. To an Australian a *digger* is a *soldier* (slang); a *station* is what we call a *ranch,* and it will be located *outback.* A *sundowner* is a *hobo;* a term for a well-liked person is *a fair dinkum bloke;* and when an Australian admires something, he may call it *wizard.* An Australian mother puts a *serviette* by your plate at the table, but a *napkin* (*diaper*) on the baby. Terms such as these are likely to be familiar to some of you because of popular songs, movies, newspaper stories, and television documentaries about Australia. The mass media familiarize us with such special terms, and will continue to do so.

Emily Kimbrough tells of an amusing difficulty she had with British English in her book *Our Hearts Were Young and Gay*. She and her young girl friend wanted to take a shower after checking into a British boarding house. They were instructed to ensure plenty of hot water by first "giving a shilling to the old geezer" located near the shower stall. After much timid inquiry and embarrassment they discovered that the *geezer* was not an elderly male custodian of the shower, but rather a *geyser*, the British term for the hot water heater. This one worked on a meter.

There are many other words which are special to British English. However, American English is making such inroads into the British vocabulary that it is difficult to present a list of words of which we can say, "These words exclusively, and not their American equivalents, are used by the British today." Nowadays the British are very likely to know the American word and to use it part of the time. Nevertheless, here is a sampling:

British Term	American Term
crisps	potato chips
chips	French fries
torch	flashlight
queue up	line up
bobby, constable	policeman
lorry	truck
caravan	trailer
on the hire system or on the "never never"	on the installment plan
lumber room	storage room
dustbin	garbage can
windscreen	windshield
boot	trunk of a car
accumulator	battery
hood	convertible top (of a car)
mudguard	fender
saloon	sedan
bonnet	hood (of a car)
snap	snapshot
an action	a lawsuit
cine shots	movie shots

Exercises

1. Any good dictionary should tell you where an English word came from. This information is found either at the beginning of an entry or at the end, depending upon the dictionary, but always it will be given within brackets. The entry may also tell what the word meant at the time it was borrowed, how it was spelled, and what its cognates, or "cousin words," are in related members of the language family. Each dictionary gives the information in an abbreviated form to save space. The symbols and abbreviations they use may vary slightly from book to book, and you should be familiar with their meanings if you are to read the etymologies (word histories) accurately. Dictionaries list many language abbreviations in the table at the front of the book. The following are among the abbreviations most often used to identify sources of English words. Look them up and list their meanings.

Am.	AS.	Dan.	Am. Fr.	Celt.	Fr.
Ar.	D.	G.	Gmc.	Goth.	Gr.
Ice.	I.E.	L.	ME.	MGr.	OFr.
ON.	Sw.	Ind.	Sem.	ONorm. Fr.	Mod. Gr.

2. Look up the word entries for the following abbreviations in the dictionary. Copy the part of the entry which tells where and when each language was current.

AS.　　　ON.　　　OFr.　　　ME.　　　LG.　　　LL.

3. List the symbols or abbreviations which your dictionary uses to tell you in the etymology that a word has been "derived from" or "taken from" another language. Then find five words in your dictionary which contain your dictionary's equivalent of *AS.* in the etymology, five words which contain *L.*, and five words which contain *ME.*

4. Read the section on etymology in the front of your dictionary. It will explain how information about a word's history is given, and it will help you interpret it. By way of an example, here is the etymology for the word *board*, taken from *Webster's Third New International Dictionary* (the entire entry is reproduced at the end of Chapter 6).

[ME *bord* piece of sawed lumber, table, shield, ship's side, border, fr. OE; akin to OHG *bort* ship's side, ON *borth* piece of sawed lumber, table, ship's side, Goth *fotubaurd* footstool, Skt *bardhaka*, *vardhaka*, adj., cutting off, n. carpenter, and perh. to Gk *perthein* to destroy]

Written out in full the entry would look something like this:

The word *board* appeared in Middle English, was spelled *bord* at that time, and meant variously "a piece of sawed lumber," "a table," "a shield," "a ship's side," and "a border." It came to Middle English from Old English and is related in meaning to the Old High German word *bort*, meaning "a ship's side"; to the Old Norse word *borth*, meaning "a piece of sawed lumber," "a table," and "ship's side"; to the Gothic word *fotubaurd*, meaning "footstool"; to the Sanskrit words *bardhaka* and *vardhaka*, with an adjective meaning of "cutting off" and a noun meaning of "carpenter"; and perhaps to the Greek word *perthein*, meaning "to destroy,"

Look up any three of the following words in your dictionary, examine the part of the entry between brackets, and explain in a sentence for each word (a) where it came from, (b) what its earliest meaning was, and (c) what its cognates are (if any).

plumb	horse	howdah	chrysanthemum
helicopter	hoyden	rogue	blond
pachyderm	psychic	tantalize	angel
house	tank	cavalier	perspective
psalm	expectorate	frangible	starve
tangerine	master	pester	staphylococcus
turban	dinosaur	sherbet	inspire
misanthrope	eclectic	tennis	piscatology
din	kowtow	caterpillar	pseudonym
mercury			

5. Make up a list of ten common words, the kind which refer to everyday objects or actions, the kind which occur most often in your speech. Look up the etymology of each in the dictionary and determine whether the word is a native or a borrowed word. If a word is listed as AS. (or OE.), consider it to be a native English word. If the word is not a native word, make a note of its origin.

Next, make a list of ten "fancy" words, the kind which you do not ordinarily use in conversation, but which you might find in reading. Follow the same procedure with these.

Last, make a list of ten specialized words. Choose words which are part of the vocabulary of a special field. Select one of these fields: war, medicine, law, art, architecture, fashion, religion, hunting, or medicine. Follow the same procedures with these words.

Examine your findings carefully and consider these questions:

- *a.* Which list, if any, has the most native words?
- *b.* Are the "fancy" words mostly native or mostly borrowed?
- *c.* Do they come mostly from just one or two languages?
- *d.* Are the specialized terms mostly native or are they mostly borrowed?
- *e.* Do they come from just a few or from many different languages?
- *f.* Can you relate any of these word origins to the cultural events or political events mentioned in this chapter?
- *g.* Out of all the thirty words, what percentage is not native English?
- *h.* What does this exercise tell you about the characteristics of native words?
- *i.* Does it tell you anything about the kinds of words which are borrowed and where they come from?

Write a paragraph summarizing your findings.

6. Here is another sampling exercise which can give you information about word borrowing. Open your dictionary at random, examine the etymology of each word on facing pages and note the earliest source for each. Some words may be native, and their origin will be noted as *AS.* or *OE.* Words which do not have this notation will be considered to be borrowed words. Tabulate your results and answer these questions about the findings:

- *a.* What percentage of words on the two pages is native?
- *b.* What percentage is borrowed from French?
- *c.* What percentage is borrowed from Latin or Greek?
- *d.* What percentage is borrowed from all other languages?
- *e.* What is the ratio of native words to borrowed words?

Compare your results with those of others in the class and discuss.

7. One way to make concrete use of your knowledge of language is to become familiar with the roots and affixes which have come to us from Greek and Latin. Knowing the meanings of these ele-

ments will help enlarge your vocabulary by enabling you to recognize parts of unfamiliar words. Many of these are listed as combining forms in the dictionary. This term means that the word component will be listed as an actual entry and will be recognizable because it begins or ends with a hyphen. Many other roots will not be listed as separate entries, and their presence and meaning must be discovered in a word's etymology.

Look up any five of the following roots in the dictionary. Copy the root definition and find one more word which contains that root. Then look up each combined form or example word in the dictionary, list the root meaning, and find one more example word containing the root.

Root	Example	Root	Example
biblio-	bible	philo-	philology
chrono-	chronicle	-pod	tripod
demos	democrat	psycho-	psychopath
dermo-	pachyderm	tele-	telephone
dyna-	dynamo	theo-	theology
geo-	geology	anima	animate
-graph, -gram	telegraph, telegram	port	portable
-logy	psychology	spiro-	respire
bio-	biology	tract	retract

8. Look up all of these combining forms (prefixes) in the dictionary and list their meanings. Find also one example word for each prefix.

Prefix	Prefix	Prefix
a-	poly-	multi-
anti-	pro-	non-
auto-	pseudo-	post-
di-	ab-	pro-
dia-	ante-	retro-
hyper-	bi-	sub-
hypo-	circum-	super-
micro-	contra-	trans-
mono-	ex-	omni-
neo-	mal-	magni-
peri-	deca-	tri-

9. Look up all of these combining forms (suffixes) in the dictionary and list their meanings. Find also one example word for each suffix.

Suffix	Suffix	Suffix
-ist	-ize	-tude
-itis	-meter	-fy
-ive	-cide	-ism

10. Paraphrase familiar quotations and proverbs by substituting for each word in the quotation appropriate defining phrases taken from the dictionary. For example:

> Bring into being grass dried for use as fodder during the time that the incandescent body of gasses about which the earth revolves is emitting light.
>
> Translation: Make hay while the sun shines.

Try it with these sentences or with some of your own. See if you can confound your parents or friends with your "dictionary proverbs."

   a. Too many cooks spoil the broth.
   b. A stitch in time saves nine.
   c. A fool and his money are soon parted.
   d. A penny saved is a penny earned.
   e. A rolling stone gathers no moss.
   f. Every cloud has a silver lining.
   g. Great oaks from little acorns grow.
   h. An apple a day keeps the doctor away.
   i. A squeaking wheel gets the most grease.
   j. Every dog has his day.
   k. If the shoe fits, wear it.
   l. Money-talks.

Try the paraphrasing with synonyms (as in "Indicate the way to my abode; I'm fatigued and I wish to retire").

11. Skim the dictionary and find five scientific or technical terms which have been formed from Greek or Latin parts.

12. The following terms appeared in a British motorcycle technical manual concerning the care and operation of the machine. What American terms and spellings would you substitute for the italicized British ones?

   a. Do not operate the machine at full speed before the end of the *running in* period.
   b. Do not let the *tyres* fall below minimum stated pressures.
   c. The lights are also controlled by the *dipper switch.*

d. Further items may be obtained by writing to the *spares stocklist.*
e. Care should be taken when *topping up* the battery.
f. If the engine has a tendency *to pink* . . . .
g. The *sparking plug* should be cleaned when *sooted.*
h. The *carburetter* adjusting screw should be turned *anti-clock-wise* . . . .
i. The *headlamp* on this *motor cycle* . . . .
j. Care should be taken to wipe off the *enamel* and the *plating* . . . .
k. The valves may need *grinding-in.*
l. *Labour* can be saved by using the *spanner* which is conveniently carried in the toolkit.

Bibliography

The following books were useful in compiling the information in this chapter. They are also recommended to the student who wishes further reading.

Baugh, Albert C. *A History of the English Language,* second edition. New York: Appleton-Century-Crofts, Inc., 1957.

Francis, W. Nelson. *The English Language: An Introduction.* New York: W. W. Norton & Company, Inc., 1965.

Greenough, James Bradstreet, and George Lyman Kittredge. *Words and Their Ways in English Speech,* New York: Beacon Press, Inc., 1962.

Jespersen, Otto. *Growth and Structure of the English Language,* ninth edition. Garden City, New York: Doubleday & Company, Inc., 1955.

Laird, Charlton. *The Miracle of Language.* Greenwich, Conn.: Premier Books, 1960.

Lloyd, Donald J., and Harry R. Warfel. *American English in Its Cultural Setting.* New York: Alfred A. Knopf, Inc., 1957.

Potter, Simeon. *Our Language.* Baltimore: Penguin Books, Inc., 1959.

Pyles, Thomas. *The Origins and Development of the English Language.* New York: Harcourt, Brace & World, Inc., 1964.

Robertson, Stuart, and Frederic G. Cassidy. *The Development of Modern English,* second edition. Englewood Cliffs, N.J.: Prentice-Hall, Inc., 1954.

Schlauch, Margaret. *The Gift of Language.* New York: Dover Publications, Inc., 1955.

Whitehall, Harold. "The English Language," *Webster's New World Dictionary of the American Language,* college edition. Cleveland: The World Publishing Company, 1959.

3

Processes of Word Creation

1. Our Inventive Language

English is nothing if not versatile. As we have seen, many words are borrowed into the language when needed. But borrowing cannot begin to satisfy the demand for the new words that our complex and expanding society requires. Happily, we have within the operation of the language itself some built-in and acquired processes which create words and extend meanings endlessly. Were we never to borrow another foreign word, root, or affix, we could get along nicely, taking care of our future word needs through the means of word creation which we already have. In this chapter we are going to identify some of these methods and show you how they work.

2. Blends

Once there was a man who was telling about an exciting experience—his car had lost traction on an icy hill and was sliding slowly to the edge of a deep dropoff. He started to say, "I was frantic!" But the word *panicky* was also on the tip of his tongue, and the sentence came out, "I was *franicky!*" He had accidentally made up a new word, a blend of *frantic* and *panicky*. Who knows? A word like this could catch on. Most such combinations are created on purpose, however, and are variously called *telescoped words, portmanteau* ("suitcase") *words,* or *blends.* A blend is a combination of parts of two words to form a third word which contains some of the meaning of each part.

48

Need a word for the meal halfway between breakfast and lunch? Use *brunch*. Lewis Carroll, author of *Alice in Wonderland*, liked to play with words in this way. He compressed *chuckle* and *snort* into *chortle*, a name used now for a special kind of a laugh. Can you tell which words have been blended to form *smog, motel, hokum, cinematography, Dixiecrat, Eurasia*, and *Medicare?* Some blends, like *anecdotage* (*anecdote* and *dotage*) are designed to amuse. Others, like *Medicare* or *Malaysia*, are seriously conceived and may be around a good while because they are words of importance to almost everyone.

Exercises

1. Using your dictionary if necessary, list the meanings of the separate parts which make up these blends:

Pulmotor	Cinerama	telecast
cosmonaut	gerrymander	infanticipate
nucleonics	Fortran	

2. Using your imagination, make up a blend of your own. Use it in a sentence designed to bring out its meaning.
3. Browse through advertisements in magazines and compile a list of blends used in brand names or advertising copy. For example: Fordomatic and Chromatone.

3. Clipping

Another common way of making a word is to shorten, or clip, a longer word. Most of the time the result will be a synonym which is often so much more convenient to use than the longer words, that the longer word will be put out of business. *Omnibus*, meaning "a vehicle of transportation," has given way to its shortened form, *bus*. *Fan*, shortened from *fanatic*, has acquired a special meaning all its own.

Apparently we tend to clip words which we use a lot, words like *bike, auto, car*, and *taxi*. This last word, by the way, was shortened from *taximeter cabriolet*. In school we shorten subjects to words like *econ, gym, math*, and *trig*. We eat *lunch* (from *luncheon*) and have a *burger* and a *shake*, or possibly a *Coke*.

Clipping is not a new process, and it is not always approved of. Jonathan Swift, who wrote in the eighteenth century, sneered at clipping as a corruption of the language. He objected to *mob* for *mobile vulgas, poss* for *positive,* and *rep* for *reputation.* He may be spinning in his grave today! Clipped words tend to be casual but very useful.

We have a variation of clipping called "back formation," a process whereby a shortened verb is made from a noun and vice versa. For example, from *percolator* came the verb *to perk,* from *emotion* came *to emote,* from television came *to televise,* and from *destruction* came *to destruct.* This last back formation was created out of the jargon of space technology and given wide circulation by a television series that dealt with espionage, adventure, and tapes that could "self-destruct." Some back formations like *televise* are accepted by everyone; others, like *enthuse,* are treated like poor relations for years and attain acceptance only because they refuse to disappear. Generally speaking, people who feel strongly that the language should give way slowly to change look down their noses at back formations. Newspaper and magazine writers coin many of these words. Ironically, the same words coined on the front page of a newspaper are often condemned as poor usage by editorialists in the inner pages.

Another special kind of clipping occurs when we make words out of initials which stand for other words. Such constructions are called *acronyms.* Their usage first became widespread during the nineteen-thirties, mainly because of the proliferation of government agencies commonly identified only by their initials (such as the WPA and CCC). World War II spawned many more of them and made the practice popular of having the acronym spell an already existent word that was also somehow appropriate (for example, WAVE for the Navy's woman's auxiliary). A more contemporary example is the Galaxy, an instrument which automates and refines the process of analyzing star fields. The individual letters making up the name *galaxy* stand for "general *a*utomatic *l*uminosity" plus *x* and *y*. The last two letters stand for the two axial coordinates of the measurement system that pins down a star image on a photograph. (The second *a* is added to make the acronym not only a pronounceable word but an appropriate one.)

Other acronyms which you might be familiar with are UN, UNICEF, NASA, CORE, CARE, VISTA, SALT, MIRV, and WAIF. Even if you had never heard of the last one, you would be able to guess that it is a charitable organization designed to help children in some way. Up to now, acronyms have always stood for longer words. VISTA, for instance, stands for Volunteers in Service to America; JOBS stands for Job Opportunities for Better Skills. But now the trend is changing, and recent "name" groups have selected titles which do not stand for any special words. Perhaps it became too much trouble. ACT, a civil-rights organization, and ENABLE, an antipoverty project, do not admit that the separate letters in their names stand for anything in particular.

Exercises

1. Make up a list of five words which have been clipped and which you use in your daily life.
2. *Radar, sonar,* and *loran* are acronyms. Check your dictionary and tell what the separate letters in each stand for.
3. Find and list two more acronyms such as *CARE* and *SEATO*.
4. Business makes good use of initial-words also, as in the words *Comsat* and *Nabisco*. Find and list three more from the business world.
5. What longer words were these clipped from: *prefab, pram, zoo, vet, combo, quotes, mum* (flower), *cat* (earth-mover)?
6. What brand name is an acronym of Fabrica Italiano Automobile Torino?
7. Make up three of your own acronyms. Let the initials stand for actual words.

4. Proper Names

Some words have been created from proper names, either of people or of places. Once these pass into the language, we are usually not aware of their origin. Still, it is true that one way to get your name perpetuated in the language is to become famous or infamous through some invention or deed. This was the case with *sandwich* (invented by the Earl of Sandwich), *guy* (originally applied to persons so tattered that they looked like the straw-stuffed figures of Guy Fawkes, a British traitor, that the English burn every November), *macadam* (invented by McAdam), and *saxophone* and *sousaphone* (invented by Mr. Sax and Mr. Sousa). Other names are imbedded in *ferris wheel, pasteurize, diesel, pullman, fahrenheit, mesmerism, filibert, calico,* and *mercerized*.

Proper names associated with clothing are *chesterfield, raglan,* and *cardigan.* From a senator and his Senate hearings came the word *McCarthyism;* from the man who jumped off the Brooklyn Bridge came a word for a suicide jump, a *brodie;* from a comic strip character came the name for a shy, timid man, a *milquetoast;* and from an unscrupulous lawyer came *shyster,* which describes the same. A long-time bachelor, newly married, is called a *benedict,* after a character in Shakespeare's *Much Ado About Nothing.* Likewise, we get *dunce* from a scholar in the Middle Ages, Duns Scotus, who ironically enough was very brilliant. Other names, and more grisly ones, are *derrick* (after a hangman) and *guillotine* (after Joseph Guillotin, a French physician who did not invent the lethal machine, but proposed its use).

Names of places also have transferred their meanings in this way. Books are bound in *morocco* leather; plates are made of *china;* sailors used to get *shanghaied; bourbon* whiskey originally was made in Bourbon County, Kentucky; men may wear *homburg* hats or eat *hamburger* (Homburg and Hamburg, Germany), and women with good figures may wear *bikinis* (a Pacific atoll where atomic bombs were tested). Notice that when a proper name joins the common vocabulary in this way, it tends to lose its capital letter after a time.

Exercises

1. Look up these words in a dictionary and explain how they acquired a meaning in our general vocabulary:

quisling	Burgundy (wine)	shrapnel	the Charleston
maverick	ritzy	cologne	mackintosh
ohm	caesarean section	turkey	blarney
silhouette	diesel	atlas	Java (coffee)

2. Names of the days of the week and the months of the year are entered in your dictionary. Check them to see which are named after people, gods, or mythical characters.

5. Compounding

Of all the methods of making words from native resources, compounding is one of the oldest and most used. You need only count the compounds on a page of the daily paper to realize how many there are. And the trend is to make more and more of them. A compound is two or more words used together to make a new word. Sometimes it will appear hyphenated, sometimes not; there is no hard and fast rule to follow. The only way to really be sure about how a compound is written is to consult a dictionary, and even dictionaries will differ.

Here are some compounds culled from newspapers: *overflight, backlash* (which gave birth to *frontlash*), *cease-fire, over-kill, free-fall, fallout, cookout, spacecraft, splash-down, wiretap, sealab, dropout, holdout, sit-in, lie-in, fly-in,* and *teach-in.* A news story reported that an Indian tribe in Washington was planning to hold a *fish-in* to publicize its claim to certain fishing rights. Other compounds, all found in one article in *Time* magazine, include *manned-space-flight, hovercraft, monorail, aero-train, turboprop, wingspan,* and *Skybus.* The good thing about compounds is that many of them need little definition because usually we already know the meanings of their separate parts.

According to the dictionary, words like the following are also compounds, even though they are not joined—*ice cream, cold war, big time* (as in the phrase "in the big time"), *retro rocket, launch pad,* and *push button.* These are called *open compounds* and are treated in the dictionary as single nouns. They may not always remain open. In the past such words have tended to evolve into hyphenated words and then into unhyphenated single words, but it is risky to generalize. *Ice cream* has been around a long time, but it is still open. So is *high school,* although attempts have been made to run it together as *highschool.* On the other hand, *spacecraft,* a comparatively recent coinage, is appearing in newspapers as one word.

Verb-adverb compounds generally appear as separate words—you can find *flyover* as a noun, but it is *fly over* as a verb; *dropout* is a noun, but *drop out* is the verb.

Compounding has been a source of new words for English ever since Anglo-Saxon times. Some of the very earliest include *camp-stede,* which meant *battlefield* (see our word *homestead*), *candel-stæf* (*candlestick*), *dēofol-sēocnis* (*devil-sickness*), *sæ-monn* (*sea-man*), *bord-weall* (*wall of shields*), and *monn-cynn* (*mankind*).

Some old words in our language are disguised compounds—words whose compound elements are no longer apparent. All of our adverbs ending with -*ly* are in this class, since the ending originally was the word *like* (*lice* in Anglo-Saxon) as in *truly* ("truth-like") and *gladly* ("glad-like"). Other disguised compounds are *answer* (*and swear*), *doff* (*do off*), *don* (*do on*), *breakfast* (literally "to break a fast"), and *good-by* ("God be with you"). Such dropping of letters and changing of pronunciation is the ultimate step in the compounding process.

Exercises

1. Skim two columns of a newspaper and list all the compound words which you find there.
2. Skim your dictionary; find and list ten open compounds, ten hyphenated compounds, and ten closed, unhyphenated compounds.
3. The following are compounds of Latin or Greek words. Check them or their components in dictionary and list the literal Latin or Greek meaning for each part of each word. Example: *stereophonic*— "three-dimensional" and "sound."

photograph	pseudonym	psychoanalysis	scutiform
seismograph	quadrangle	Rosicrucian	rotogravure
catapult	subpoena	helioscope	kleptomania

4. The following compounds are written here as open and unhyphenated. Write them as you think they should be written; then check each with several dictionaries to see how close you came and whether the dictionary-makers agree with each other.

mad cap	mail bag	race course	steeple chase
smash up	shoe shine	wind ward	sledge hammer
stage coach	jet powered	second hand	square bracket
stereo chemistry	stiff necked	battle ground	by pass

5. How many noun-plus-noun compounds can you list? Use the dictionary if it helps. Examples: *airline, horsehide.*
6. How many adjective-plus-noun compounds can you list? Examples: *blackboard, redhead.*
7. How many verb-plus-adverb compounds can you list? Examples: *run-in, setup, make-up.*
8. Try to find at least five hyphenated compounds of three or more words.

6. Metaphor

Large numbers of word meanings are created through the process of metaphor. What this process means is that words already in the language are given additional meaning through an imaginative extension of their literal sense. For example, after World War II many navy ships were no longer needed for immediate use—yet they were far too expensive to scrap. Besides, they might be needed again at some future date. The government decided that the ships should be deactivated, taken out of commission, and preserved in storage. Since the ships were too large to wrap in brown paper and put on a shelf, all vital parts and machinery were coated with thick grease, and anything else which might rust or otherwise deteriorate was sprayed with a thin coat of rubbery plastic for protection. The name given to this operation was *mothballing*, although the mothball had nothing to do with this kind of storage. Since then we have read from time to time in the newspapers of "the mothball fleet," of "putting ships in mothballs," or even of "demothballing" ships. Obviously, the word *mothball* has taken on a new and extra meaning, one which gives us a quick and clever way of saying that the ships are being kept in a state of preservation.

In a way, a metaphor is like a puzzle—it finds one common point of likeness between two things or ideas which are basically different. In this case the common likeness was contained in the idea of preservation, and this idea was borrowed in the "mothball" metaphor.

The liking we have for finding figurative meanings may actually result in new words and word combinations: *brainwashing* for mental torture or indoctrination, *hatchet job* for an act of defamation or slander, *sneaker* for a tennis shoe, *coffin nail* for a cigarette, *globetrotter* for a world traveler, *brain trust* for a group of expert advisers, *egghead* for an intellectual, *cold-shoulder* for a verb meaning "to neglect or to be unfriendly," *snow job* for a verbal attempt to impress and *cold war* for a conflict short of violence. Metaphors like these can present ridiculous pictures if taken literally. To understand them you must stretch your imagination and find the comparison which makes the word's meaning come through.

Most metaphors simply add new meanings to words already established. In fact, there is scarcely an old, long-established word that does not have metaphorical meanings added to its basic literal senses. Thus, *summit*, which literally means "a peak, or point of highest elevation," has acquired the metaphorical meaning of "a meeting between chiefs of government." *Butter* has acquired the meaning of "to flatter grossly"; and *butcher*, which basically meant "one who kills animals," now additionally means "a person guilty of cruel and indiscriminate slaughter." Likewise, *crack* has acquired the meaning of "to become unsound mentally" and *hurdle* has acquired the meaning of "to master a difficulty." From the literal meaning of *nail*, "to fasten together with nails," has been derived a figurative meaning, "to hold, bind; hence catch, as a thief." Sometimes the metaphorical meaning is so strong that it comes to mind more quickly than the basic or literal meaning.

We create and use metaphor words to help make our speech and writing fresher and more effective. We read in the papers of towns which *mushroom* and have *bedroom* districts; we tell of public opinion which *simmers* and *boils*, of executives who are *tied up* and of clients who *stew* in reception rooms, of actors who *milk* their audiences for laughs or *drain* them of emotion.

What ultimately happens with many metaphor words is that they become so commonplace that we no longer see the figurative meaning in them. You might say that when a dead metaphor goes unrecognized, the word is a success—it has gotten a lot of use. But in another sense, the word is a failure, for it has lost part of its impact.

Among the deadest and oldest metaphors are those which borrow from parts of the human anatomy: the *mouth* of a river, the *foot* of a mountain, the long *arm* of the law, the *mind's* eye, the *hands* and *face* of a clock, the *brow* of a hill, the *tongue* of flame, the *teeth* of the gale. We also have unconscious metaphors when we use expressions like "brake shoes," "the leaves of a book," "feeling blue," "seeing red," "the key to the puzzle," and "airing our troubles." There are hundreds of others; all were once fresh and new. Now when we use them we scarcely realize that they are meanings which have been created through extensions of earlier meanings of words.

Exercises

1. Explain both the literal and figurative meanings in these metaphors:

He is a *turncoat* trying to return from Red China.

From discoveries of scientists perfecting the atom bomb have come *spin-offs* important to the field of medicine.

The Sino-Soviet split has *polarized* the Japanese left wing.

The *upshot* of the discussion was that he quit his job.

Opponents declared that the talk was a *smoke screen* designed to obscure the real evils of substandard housing.

We had a real *blast* last night.

She certainly has a *sunny disposition*.

It is time that we did something about *down-at-the-heels* housing.

They had parted six months earlier, but he was still *carrying a torch*.

Negotiations between the two parties were *snagged* over the question of missile site inspection.

The President spent most of the interview time *sparring* with reporters, parrying those questions which he did not want to answer.

Because it was a holiday, only a *skeleton* crew was on duty.

2. For each of the following words write two sentences, one illustrating the literal meaning of the word, the other illustrating the metaphorical meaning. Use the dictionary if help is needed.

jungle	oasis	cool	flower	satellite
stomach	sniping	splinter	lobby	crystallize

3. Sometimes proper names of well-known people and places acquire a metaphorical meaning. For example, to call someone a *Jonah* suggests that he is bad luck. To understand the use of the word in this sense you must be familiar enough with the story of the biblical Jonah to make the association. In the following sentences the italicized names are used in a similar metaphorical way. Look up each in your dictionary and be ready to explain how the metaphorical meaning is derived.

Standing before the minister, taking the vows of marriage, I realized that I was about to cross my *Rubicon*.

They laughed at this modern-day *Cassandra* when she warned that Castro was going to turn Cuba into a Communist state.

The tasks before me looked *Herculean*.

He was a *colossus* standing there, dominating the room with his size.

In the depths of my despair I felt that I had reached my *Gethsemane*.

Playing middle-linebacker, he was a *Gibralter* on defense.

4. Try to think of a similar word and write a sentence illustrating its metaphoric use.

5. Using your dictionary for help if necessary, discuss the metaphorical sense of each of these words.

doormat	sleeper	spearhead	cultivate
crisp	carpet	ice	frame
freeze	cat	fish	sea
read	chisel	screen	front

6.   Many slang words are created through a process of metaphor. In fact, the imaginative suggestion of resemblances is what we chiefly find intriguing about slang. The very same could be said for jargon, the lingo which people in particular occupations devise and use in their work. For example, automobile stylists use words like these: *dogleg*—the bend in the windshield post projecting into the front door opening; *greenhouse*—the upper part of the car, including the glass area; *tuned in*—describing a man who knows what he is doing; *blister*—bump over the wheel for clearance.

Can you decipher the following paragraph, written by a hot-rodder? Can you explain the metaphors which are present in the italicized words?

> Look at the *pots* on that rig. With that *bent eight* she'll really get up and go. And check the *rake*, man. It's really low. Hear those *binders?* Really took some off the *skins,* eh?

7.   The following terms and definitions are part of the special language which surfers use. Pick out those terms which seem to be derived through metaphor and explain how they might have been created.

coffin: Riding a wave while lying flat on a board, with arms folded across the chest.

hot dogger: A surfer skilled at stunts.

Quasimodo: Riding crouched on a board, with one arm forward, one back.

wipe-out: A fall off of a surfboard.

soup: The foamy part of a wave.

hodad: An objectionable, nonsurfing hanger-on.

8.   List two slang words created from metaphor and explain their figurative meaning.

9.   List some animal names or derivatives which carry metaphorical meanings and demonstrate their use in sentences. Example: "He *wolfed* his food."

10.   How many ways are there for a sports writer to say that Podunk defeated Waybelow Normal in an athletic contest? Re-

porters of sporting events are constantly pressed to find new and colorful verbs to catch the reader's flagging attention. In spite of their efforts, the supply of fresh words grows thin, and certain metaphor verbs, which at first must have been vivid, have now become so commonplace in sports stories that we are scarcely aware of their imaginative content. Do you recognize the verbs in the following headlines as metaphors? If not, it is because their overuse has deadened their meaning. Just for fun, visualize the action which would be going on if each of the verbs were taken literally!

Kicking Game Kills OSU

Troy Clobbers Badgers, 26–6

Tars Dump Bucks, 14–3

Bears Nudge UW, 17–14

Haller's 2 Homers Spark SF

Steers Romp, 33–7

Vandals Rap Sparts, 17–7

LSU Cooks Rice, 42–14

Navy Sinks Army 6–0

Hawkeyes Burst Beaver Bubble

Wildcats Rip Indiana, 20–0

Whiff Mark Falls; Dodgers Roll

Bearcats Nip Nevada, 9–6

Chisox Trip Yanks Twice

Spartans Pound Penn State, 23–0

Dodgers Bag 10th Straight

Tide Blasts Wave, 27–0

Birds Notch 8th in Row

In what way do the scores in these headlines determine the choice of verb? Which team names were created metaphorically? Which team name is a blend? What is inappropriate about the verb in the headline "Tide Blasts Wave"? What would you substitute for the verb?

11. Writers use metaphor to say things in memorable ways. The following passage from Shakespeare's *Hamlet* occurs when Prince Hamlet, knowing that two courtiers are trying to get information from him, asks them if they know how to play a recorder (a slender wind instrument). When they reply that they have not the skill to play one, Hamlet replies:

> Why, look you now, how unworthy a thing you make of me! You would play upon me; you would seem to know my stops; you would pluck out the heart of my mystery; you would sound me from my lowest note to the top of my compass; and there is much music, excellent voice, in this little organ, yet cannot you make it speak. 'Sblood, do you think I am easier to be played on than a pipe? Call me what instrument you will, though you can fret me, you cannot play upon me.

Read the passage again carefully and then be prepared to discuss these questions: What major comparison is being made throughout the passage? Which words in the passage carry both literal and figurative (metaphoric) meanings at the same time?

7.   Conversion

Can you identify the different functions of the word *round* in these sentences?

> He was knocked out in the first round.
> Round the number off to the nearest tenth.
> The neighbors gathered round our barbecue.
> The moon was bright and round.
> People came from all the country round.

In each sentence *round* is used as a different part of speech— noun, verb, preposition, adjective, and adverb—illustrating another way by which the meanings of words are increased. The process is called *conversion*, or *functional shift*, and it names a tendency we have of making nouns out of our verbs, verbs out of our nouns, and of generally testing words out in all functioning positions. The process of conversion dates back to the Middle English period. Any number of our older words will display at least verb and noun meanings, and often others as well. They have been gradually added to the words as time has passed. Can you think quickly of noun and verb meanings for these words: *rough, swing, troop, shot, pipe, master, ice, hail, draw, grip, flower, drop, square, dent, cure, comb, case, can,* and *bump?*

Here are some verbs which have been made from nouns:

> They *gifted* him with a watch.
> We *duetted* on "Indian Love Call."
> Bill *chaired* the meeting.
> She *flatted* her last note.
> Let us *service* your car.

And here are some nouns which have been made from verb-adverb combinations such as *to drive in:*

> Our company has a yearly *turnover* of personnel.
> Let's get on with the *clean-up.*
> How do you like our new *setup?*
> My car needs a big *overhaul.*
> Take the next *turnout* to the right.

Even the simple word *go* has acquired many more meanings through the years than just the verb idea. The unabridged dictionary lists ten different meanings of the word as a noun, including contexts such as "to have a go at it," "no go," and "on the go." To these we can now add the context from space research jargon, "All systems are go!"

Exercises

1. Browse through the dictionary; find and list two words which can be used as three parts of speech.

2. In what order or arrangement does your dictionary list conversion meanings? (Is the verb meaning always listed first? Are the verb and noun meanings all mixed up together? Are they listed as separate entries?)

8. Onomatopoeia and Reduplication

A relatively few words have been created through *onomatopoeia,* or imitation of sound. A word of this kind has been created directly from the sound it names. The process gives us words (and sounds) like *murmur, cluck, clack, cock-a-doodle-doo, buzz, whoop, bow-wow, gurgle,* and *gargle* (for an interesting origin of this word, see *gargoyle*). Other imitative words are *wham, bam, pow, tinkle,* and *zowie*—all indispensable to the action in the comic strips.

Another group of words comes to us through a sound process called *reduplication.* These words repeat themselves with little or no change. Somehow, the repetition of the sound is satisfying to the ear; or perhaps we like the emphasis it gives. At any rate, we have a fair number of curiosities in the language like *hoity-toity, spic-and-span, shilly-shally, fiddle-faddle, mishmash,* and *willy-nilly* (which long ago was given as *will I nill I*).

In World War II *hubba hubba* was a popular reduplication. No one knew exactly what it meant or where it came from. Generally, it was a sign of enthusiasm, but sometimes it was just something a squad of soldiers said automatically when given the command "At ease." Perhaps it came from an imitation of the sound made by a group of people talking. Some lesser-known reduplications are *miz-maze* (a maze), *fingle-fangle* (it meant "a trifle," but is now obsolete), *snick-and-snee* ("fighting with knives," also obsolete), and *huggermugger* (which means "secrecy").

9. Affixing

One of the most flexible ways of creating words is by affixing, which means attaching beginnings (prefixes) or endings (suffixes) to base words. We have already seen how extensively this method works with Greek and Latin prefixes such as *anti-*, *ante-*, *re-*, *mono-*, and the like. Here are other useful affixes.

Suffix	Example	Example
-er	worker	learner
-ette	flannelette	dinette
-ee	enrollee	payee
-ize	verbalize	minimize
-ation	verbalization	miniaturization
-ish	Spanish	foolish
-ess	poetess	goddess
-ness	sickness	goodness
-dom	filmdom	kingdom
-less	meatless	worthless
-able	readable	singable
-ly	dependably	worthlessly
-ry	bigotry	cookery
-ite	Salemite	trailerite
-ate	activate	pollenate
-ster	teamster	punster
-wise	endwise	otherwise

Prefix	Example	Example
de-	debark	decentralize
mis-	misplace	misdoubt
un-	unfit	uncharming
be-	become	bestow

Exercises

1. Look up in the dictionary each of the prefixes and suffixes listed in the previous section and write out their meanings. For each affix list one more word example.

2. Adjectives can be formed with *-able, -al, -er, -ic, -istic, -ive, -ary, -ible, -ish, -less, -ous, -ful, -est, -ian.* Using selected endings from this list, make adjectives out of the following words. You will need to drop or change some present endings in order to add the others.

Spain	care	expend	fancy
horror	future	rest	direct
trim	discretion	person	minimum
alcohol	panorama	wonder	thank
fine	cannibal	sense	industry
small	match	method	mix
parsimony	crustacean	taxonomy	antidisestablish-
lexicography	Shaw	Panama	mentarianism

3. Form negatives for each of the following words by adding one of these prefixes: *non-, ir-, il-, un-, im-, dis-, in-.*

elastic	symmetrical	resident	rational
reducible	entity	probable	material
partial	clement	comparable	equivocal
standard	fettered	seat	engage
legitimate	modest	palpable	corruptible
direction	finite	service	penetrable

4. Both *inflammable* and *irregardless* have been condemned as words with unnecessary prefixes, since *flammable* and *regardless* carry the same meaning. Find out all you can about the origin of these words in your unabridged dictionary and discuss (a) how each word came into being and (b) the relative merits of each.

Review Exercises

1. Using conversion, make up sentences illustrating how names for parts of the body can be shifted to other parts of speech. Example: "He *faced* the music."

2. Using conversion, make up sentences illustrating how names for objects found in a room can be shifted to other parts of speech. Example: "He *tabled* the motion."

3. Using the dictionary if necessary, name the method or methods of word formation by which the italicized words in the following sentences were created.

    a. I am studying to be an *oceanographer.*
    b. That kind of work takes a lot of *know-how.*
    c. Last year we had a *flu* epidemic.
    d. Chapter titles should be put in *quotes.*
    e. Twenty miles is a long way to *commute* each day.

f.   Space experimentation is under the control of *NASA*.

g.   She claims to be an *antidesegregationist*.

h.   How are you fixed *moneywise?*

i.   Bedlam broke out on the third floor of the *dorm*.

j.   The tablecloths were made of *damask*.

k.   A slang name for a tourist is *rubbernecker*.

l.   Jim *upped* the price yesterday.

m.   My favorite flowers are *snapdragons* and *mums*.

n.   Our school building plans call for a *cafetorium*.

o.   The jet did a *flyby* at 800 miles per hour.

p.   Hold the presses! I have an *exclusive*.

q.   We can *airfreight* the package very cheaply.

r.   The *phone* is out of order.

s.   Her clothes were cheap and *tawdry*.

t.   Can you take a *fix* on my position.

u.   Let's *weekend* in the country.

v.   The approach to the problem was *quixotic*.

w.   We will meet when the **hurly-burly** is done, over by the **hurdy-gurdy**.

x.   They claimed that society was a *hotbed* of communists.

y.   Why don't you quit talking? You're just *spinning your wheels*.

z.   When secret operative 70345 lost his *cover*, his usefulness was over.

4.   A type of aircraft is known variously as a *helicopter*, a *copter*, and a *chopper*. Explain the probable process of word formation in each name.

5.   Have you ever noticed that some words never or rarely appear without a prefix, and have you ever wondered what would happen if you dropped the prefix and made a clipped word out of it? For example:

> "You're uncouth!"
> "I am not. I'm just as couth as you are!"

Here is your chance to coin some new meanings and put them into circulation. The following words are used primarily in their affixed forms; without affixes they are nonexistent or rare. Drop the prefix from each and use the resulting word in a sentence so as to bring out its nonprefixed meaning. You will have to use the dictionary to arrive at the meaning for most of these.

unkempt	implacable	disdainful
inept	inane	insipid
nonplussed	incorrigible	nondescript
impeccable	intrepid	inscrutable

6. Someone once said, "Every language is a dictionary of faded metaphor." Write a paragraph explaining with examples why this statement is true.

7. Can the trademark name of a product pass into the language as a common noun? Yes, and strange as it may sound at first, that is one kind of success the sellers of products wish to avoid. Once the brand name of a product, *linoleum*, for example, has been accepted by the public as a generic name for all similar products, then its special trademark identification has been destroyed. Which do you say, "vacuum bottle" or "thermos bottle"? *Vacuum* is the generic name, but *thermos*, the trademark name, is a popular designation for all vacuum bottles, and a court has ruled that the word *thermos* may legally be used uncapitalized as a common noun. Another manufacturer has been having similar problems with its famous Scotch Tape. In order to prevent the adoption of the trademark as a common noun, the manufacturer has been careful in recent years to advertise Scotch Brand Cellophane Tape, thus coupling the brand name with the generic name of the product.

Here are some famous brand names which may or may not appear in the dictionary as common nouns. Look them up to see if they are there and to determine their status.

Kodak	Lanolin	Shredded Wheat
Cellophane	Kleenex	Band-Aid
Escalator	Jello	Zipper
Dynel	Kerosene	Vaseline
Aspirin	Deep Freeze	Frigidaire

8. Recently, James Lewis, a veteran entertainer, sued a network for one million dollars because the network named a T.V. program "Hootenanny" without his permission. Lewis maintained that he invented a musical device and coined the word *hootenanny* to describe it way back in 1935. He added that the word gained a secondary meaning as a name for his act, and that his act has been decreased in value because of the T.V. program with the same name. How would you settle this question if you were a judge? What does

the most recent unabridged dictionary say about the word *hoote-nanny?*

Bibliography

The following books were useful in compiling the information in this chapter. They are also recommended to the student who wishes further reading.

Bryant, Margaret M. *Modern English and Its Heritage*, New York: The Macmillan Company, 1949.

Mencken, H. L. *The American Language*, abridged by Raven I. McDavid, Jr., with the assistance of David W. Maurer. New York: Alfred A. Knopf, Inc., 1963.

Pyles, Thomas. *Words and Ways of American English*. New York: Random House, Inc., 1952.

4

Words and Their Meanings

1. Symbols and Referents

Jonathan Swift in *Gulliver's Travels* introduced the reader to a scheme for doing away with the necessity for words. Since words are but symbols for things, it might be more convenient, says Swift, for men to carry around with them the things which they want to talk about. Instead of talking, they would merely point to the objects under discussion. In the long run, such an innovation would save wear and tear on their lungs and vocal cords. Here are more details in his own words:

> Many of the most learned and wise adhere to the new scheme of expressing themselves by things, which hath only this inconvenience attending it, that if a man's business be very great, and of various kinds, he must be obliged in proportion to carry a greater bundle of things upon his back, unless he can afford one or two strong servants to attend him. I have often beheld two of these sages almost sinking under the weight of their packs, like pedlars among us; who, when they met in the streets, would lay down their loads, open their sacks, and hold conversation for an hour together; then put up their implements, help each other to resume their burdens, and take their leave.

Fortunately, Swift's tongue-in-cheek proposal did not catch on. Otherwise, the man with the biggest vocabulary would be the man with the largest warehouse! And aside from the logistical problems of transportation and supply, there is another matter to be settled—what objects do you carry with you to represent words like *honor, logic, prestige,* and *run?*

67

Swift's satiric passage helps us realize what useful symbols words are. With noises made with the aid of our lungs, vocal cords, teeth, tongues, and mouths or with squiggly marks made with pen on paper, we can communicate with one another about anything under the sun. Words work as symbols because people agree to accept them as standing for objects or concepts known to them through their experience. We use the word *referents* for these ideas, feelings, or things for which words stand. Without a referent, a symbol has no meaning. *Magazine* is a word to us because we have a common understanding that it is a symbol for a particular referent in our experience. If the dictionary records and defines this word, its status as a symbol is verified and its meaning (as most of us understand it) is given. The definition must be inclusive enough to take in the characteristics of all magazines, and it must be specific enough to exclude those referents which may resemble magazines but are not. And if the word has more than one referent, the dictionary must carefully distinguish among them.

Some referents for words exist in the physical world and are the kinds of objects which Swift would have us carry around in packs on our backs: books, houses, cars, chairs, trees. Referents like these we can see, touch, hear, or smell, and their meanings are called *concrete*. It is comparatively easy to agree upon the meanings of their symbols because we experience them through our physical senses. As S. I. Hayakawa says, the best way to define a word is to point to the object which it represents.[1]

But other referents for words exist only in our minds—ideas such as love, friendship, work, see, and study. Ideas which we cannot point to are symbolized by words which convey *abstract* meanings. Because we cannot agree upon their meanings simply by examining their physical referents, they may not be so easily defined as words with concrete meanings. Some abstract words have become symbols for whole political-social philosophies—*communism, capitalism, socialism, welfare state, democracy, Americanism, liberal, conservative*—and their meanings have become so varied and complex that complete agreement on their definitions is virtually impossible.

---

[1] For a complete discussion of many of the ideas expressed in this chapter, see S. I. Hayakawa's *Language in Thought and Action* (New York: Harcourt, Brace & World, Inc., 1964).

Even the dictionary, though it is the best available source for assessing word meaning, will not be able to make the referents of many abstract words crystal clear. What are the dictionary's limitations? For one thing, it must attempt to define symbols with other symbols (or words with other words), which is a poor substitute for conveying the meaning of a referent through firsthand experience. Reading about what the word *bicycle* means is not as satisfactory as actually seeing, examining, and riding a bicycle.

Another limitation is that the dictionary cannot possibly say all that there is to say about any word. It is restricted by considerations of time, money, and space to general statements designed to encompass all important areas of the word's meaning. Much specific information must be left out of definitions.

A third limitation will be discussed in the next section—the fact that words can carry emotional as well as informative meaning, but that the dictionary usually discusses only the latter.

Exercises

1. Letters or combinations of letters are symbols for sounds; words are symbols for things or ideas. But they are not the only symbols which are meaningful to us in our lives. What do these symbolize to you?

a.	the American flag	f.	a dollar bill
b.	a policeman's badge	g.	military ribbons
c.	a wedding ring	h.	a cross
d.	a skull and crossbone	i.	a swastika
e.	a black leather jacket	j.	a Rolls Royce

How did these become symbols? Can you think of other symbols? Make a list to add to the symbols above.

2. Consider the following information and then answer the questions below.

ombudsman: This is a Scandinavian word designating a public official who investigates complaints of the people against the government. Some people in England and the U.S. feel that their governments need such an official.

tsunamis: This is a Japanese word designating a seismic sea wave. Some scientists consider it to be a more accurate term than our *tidal wave*.

supercalifragilisticexpialidocius: This was coined for use in a popular song in the movie *Mary Poppins*.

soshadent: This is a word coined on the spur of the moment by the authors to describe a student who is more interested in social affairs than studies.

frenetic: The dictionary says that this means "frenzied" or "frantic."

a. Which of these do you consider to be words in English?
b. Which does not have a referent listed for it? Can you supply it?
c. Is *supercalifragilisticexpialidocius* likely to appear in the dictionary? Under what conditions?
d. What would have to happen before *soshadent, ombudsman,* and *tsunamis* became acceptable English word symbols?
e. Which presently unlisted words have the best chance of eventually appearing in an English dictionary? Why?
f. What criteria did *frenetic* meet to win its place in the dictionary?
g. Must a word appear in a dictionary before it can be considered a word?
h. Look up *nonce word* in your dictionary. Which word in the list does this definition apply to?

3. The word *normalcy* was apparently coined by President Harding, who used it, probably unintentionally, in a speech suggesting that the country should "return to normalcy." Although we already had a good word, *normality*, for the meaning, *normalcy* is today included in the dictionary as a word. What does this fact suggest about the reasons that certain words gain acceptance?

4. Which of these symbols have concrete referents; which have abstract referents?

soldier	honor	patriotism	tank
spirit	traffic	house	Jim
politics	dictionary	tree	animal

5. Word symbols vary in specificity as well as in concreteness and abstractness. Some words are very general, while others are quite specific. The more specific the symbol, the easier it is to agree upon its referent. For example:

> Most general—food.
> Less general—pastry.
> More specific—pie.
> Most specific—mince pie.

Sometimes it is convenient for us to use words with general meanings; sometimes it is necessary to use very specific words. Everyone should be aware that he has a choice in the matter and use the word which does the job best. Can you arrange these lists of words in order from the most general to the most specific?

a. printed material, *Mad* magazine, periodical, magazine.

b. quadruped, animal, horse, Black Beauty.

c. art film, entertainment, movie, *La Dolce Vita.*

d. Bill Jones, living creature, person, man.

e. '51 Ford, jalopy, transportation, Old Betsy.

f. Lincoln High, building, high school, institution.

6. Dictionaries use both specific and general words when defining word entries. Often the first noun in a definition is a more general word than the word which is being defined, as in the following examples. Can you explain why?

pie: A dessert with a baked crust and various fillings.

pigment: A substance that imparts black or white or a color to other materials.

quandary: A state of perplexity or doubt.

What specific nouns are in these entries? What is their function?

2.   Denotation and Connotation

Normally, when we talk about the meaning of a word, we are speaking of what we call its *denotation,* the thing or idea which it "points to." This is the meaning which we find primarily listed in the dictionary entry. For example, here is the dictionary denotation for a fish called the *smelt:* "a small, silvery food fish." You might say that this is the basic meaning of the word. But some words, many words, carry extra freight—meanings which are not included in the denotation but which are suggested by the words. Read the following news story, which appeared a few years ago, and see if you agree.

Of all the products sold in the United States the names for commercial fish are the poorest and hurt fish sales, according to a New York marketing researcher.

"Names like smelt, weakfish, and croaker contribute to the seafood industry's lack of success in reaching full sales potential," says James M. Vicary, president of the Trademark Management Institute, Inc.

"Evidently, people in the industry take these names for granted, despite their inappropriate connotations for the average consumer," says the man whose business it is to make his clients' products acceptable to everybody.

The three names given above are by no means isolated examples, Mr. Vicary says. For other examples, he gives blowfish, grunt, scrod, bullhead, cusk, hardhead, snapper, cigarhead, flounder, hogchoker, snook, crappie, fluke, mussel, squid, goggle-eye, pigfish, and sucker.

"The fish industry might well borrow from the example of other industries which sell goods to the consumer," adds Mr. Vicary.

"When a brand name or trademark develops unfavorable associations beyond correction by product changes or advertising, manufacturers are quick to rid themselves of the offending name.

"In the case of fish, so many names are involved as to require a large-scale renaming program." [1]

Even though we can agree with William Shakespeare that "a rose by any other name would smell as sweet," most of us will concede that the *connotation*, or suggestive power of a word, can rouse certain feelings in us about the referent which is symbolized. These feelings may not give an accurate representation of the denoted object, but they can often move us to action by their very strength. Or to put it simply, if certain things had pleasanter-sounding names, we might be more inclined to like them, even though the name really has nothing to do with the thing symbolized.

When water pollution became a pressing national problem and engaged the attention of a national conference, a guest speaker from the League of Women Voters suggested that the word *stink* be used to create public support for the pollution fight. She cited an instance of its successful use in Beaumont, Texas, which had a pollution problem: "In desperation they adopted the slogan 'Beaumont is beautiful, but it stinks!' This shock treatment worked!"

---

[1] Reprinted by permission from *The Christian Science Monitor*, © 1961. The Christian Science Publishing Society. All rights reserved.

Another speaker at the same conference had this to say about the word:

> Some people think it is not a nice word. To me it is a working word: it has impact. Nice words, like nice guys, as Leo Durocher once said, don't win. Without *stink,* it might be said that we would have very little pollution control.

Moral: If you want to move people to action—whether it be to buy fish or to clean up rivers and harbors—use words which will create the kind of emotional effect you desire, words which carry a high degree of connotative meaning.

Since dictionary definitions do not normally deal with connotations, we should be aware that words do have this kind of meaning for us. We encounter these charged words frequently in our listening and reading. Advertising, in particular, makes skillful use of words to impress us favorably with the advertised products. The key words in many ads are those which have little denotative meaning (sometimes none) but a great deal of connotative meaning. These key words may sound impressively scientific or they may suggest delightful experiences, neither of which may have any relevance to the product. For example, here are some sentences culled from advertising. As you read them, ask yourself the following questions: (a) What is the denotation of the italicized words? (b) What is their connotation? (c) What feeling about the product is the connotation designed to give?

> Our smoke is drawn to your lips through *pure, activated* charcoal.
>
> Try the soap crystals now *activated* for whiter washing.
>
> Now, at last, a soap which has *turbo-foam!*
>
> It is the only stereo with *astro-sonic* sound.
>
> Our hair dressing is water-active—don't use any more of that *greasy kid-stuff!*
>
> The cigarette that is *springtime fresh.*
>
> Come in and see our *color-crafted* TV.
>
> Our soap is superior because it has a *bacteria-static* agent.
>
> The hair spray that is *wickedly glamorous.*
>
> Use the spray with a *flexible hold*—the one with the *magic* ingredient *vitrol D.*
>
> For the eternal peace and security of your loved ones, arrange with *Memorial Gardens* to purchase a *Family Estate.*

> Why use *greases, goops,* and *gunks* on your hair when our *styling gel* is available?
>
> It's the *sassy* drink.
>
> The only ballpoint pen with a solid brass *nose cone.*
>
> It gives your hair *hidden magic.*

Obviously, words like these are designed not to inform us, but to impress us. Advertising copywriters know the value of connotation and they make it work for their clients.

Of course, words with connotative meaning are not the exclusive property of the advertising industry. Many, many words which occur as we go through the business of speaking, reading, listening, and writing may have some degree of emotional charge for us. Their connotations will vary from person to person, depending upon each person's past experiences with the words or their referents. To Charlie Stones, a Caucasian, the word *black* denotes a color, but to Gene Lewis, a Negro, it carries a world of connotation which far overshadows any meaning which the denotation has for him. The same is true for him of the word *Negro* itself. Recently in one of our cities, a department store used a different color designation for each floor and named the color in four languages. One floor had *black, noir* (French), *nero* (Italian), and *negro* (Spanish). The NAACP objected to this last word and asked that the designation be changed.

In a lesser degree each of us has certain words which carry connotative, nondictionary meaning. To a soldier overseas, it might be the word *home,* which in addition to its dictionary definition, may carry all these meanings: "seeing my girl friend," "eating home cooking," "wearing civilian clothes," "driving my old car," "the house at 175 Fifth Street," "my room," "my special chair," "messing around," and so on. Likewise, the youngster who had nightmares three nights in a row after viewing a certain horror movie may never hear the word *Dracula* thereafter without experiencing a slight uneasiness. When the referent for a word has acquired some importance in our experience, it is apt to have connotative meaning for us.

Civil rights, for instance, will carry a variety of emotional meanings for many people, depending upon their place of residence, their cultural heritage, the color of their skins, their economic status, and their political views. Why? Because they have become emotionally involved with the ideas which the term stands for. Not all of us necessarily react in the same way to a given word, or to the same degree. What connotations might *atomic* have for each of these?

1. A scientist working in a project to develop industrial uses for nuclear power.
2. A sailor in a nuclear submarine.
3. A Japanese resident of Hiroshima.
4. The leader of Red China.

Some of us are thin-skinned enough to be affected by the connotations suggested by different levels of English usage, apart from the meanings in the word. You have probably heard a remark like this: "He's stuck-up. All he ever uses is fancy, two-dollar words." Do the words in the following paragraph sound fancy or affected to you, or do they seem clever, impressive, and amusing? Whichever way you feel about them, that will be the connotation they carry for you.

> I tried to envision the rival patterns of ratiocination. I could be sure that Marciano, a kind, quiet, imperturbable fellow, would plan to go after Moore and make him fight continuously until he tired enough to become an accessible target. After that, he would expect concussion to accentuate exhaustion and exhaustion to facilitate concussion, until Moore came away from his consciousness.
> —A. J. Liebling, *The Sweet Science*

At the other extreme are the connotations associated with nonstandard usage. If we are used to speaking a standard dialect, we will be aware of nonstandard expressions used by other people. What attitudes toward the speaker do the italicized words in the following extract help form in your mind?

> Tom's *most* well now, and got his bullet around his neck on a watchguard for a watch, and is always seeing what time it is, and so there *ain't* nothing more to write about, and I am *rotten* glad of it, because if *I'd a knowed* what a trouble it was to make a book I wouldn't *a' tackled* it, and *ain't a-going* to no more.
> —Mark Twain, *The Adventures of Huckleberry Finn*

People who are sophisticated in the use of language know that the large number of synonyms in English provides a choice of words with varying connotations. Some words are neutral in their coloring, and have no connotations; some have pleasant connotations; and some have unpleasant ones. Thus, a person can be described as talkative, articulate, gossipy, garrulous, rambling, fluent, gabby, or mouthy, depending upon the impression one wishes to create about him. Synonyms like these are not exact duplications of meaning, certainly, but their denotations are roughly the same. The differences among them are in the shades of meaning created in part by the connotations.

The most important value of knowing about connotation is that you can be on the alert, when necessary, for words which are being used primarily for their *affective* (or *emotional*) impact rather than for their informative value. The world is full of people who are using words to influence us in one way or another, whether through suggestions that we buy certain products, vote for certain people or measures, or live our lives in particular ways. These attempts to influence us are not necessarily wrong. But we should be aware, when we let words influence our behavior and thinking, of the part which connotation may play in the process.

Exercises

1. Have you noticed that names of modern car models seem to be chosen for the images which the names project? Here are a few examples:

Name	Connotation
Mustang	suggests a spirited, fast, small animal
Grand Prix	conjures up the world of European sports car racing
GTO, XKE, LTD	"letter" names may or may not stand for other words, but letters alone are sufficient to suggest experimental models, secret designs, scientific refinements
Riviera	expensive resorts, high living, money, high fashion

Make a list of all the other car model names you can think of, classify them into categories like those already suggested or into others, and discuss their connotations.

2.   Manufacturers choose the names of their products with care. They know that the right name can motivate a customer to buy. Here are a few brand names. What connotations are built into each?

Sprite	Marlborough	Cheer	Gleem	Bold
Jade East	Green Giant	Joy	Crest	Raid

Find other names from advertising and discuss the connotations they carry.

3.   Here are two ads in which the use of connotation is particularly prominent. In both ads the information given is less important than the feeling to be created. Read them and answer the questions following each.

> Nothing's as slim, trim, and tapered as a British "brolly" (umbrella, that is). Unless it's McGregor's new "Brolly" Look. Makes a man ten feet tall! And what colors! Deep new Mystic. Spirited new Scotch. This is the flash look for Fall. The look for the young-man clan.

What color is "Mystic"? What color is "Scotch"? What connotation is "brolly" supposed to hold for the reader? What other words in this ad carry connotation? Which group is the ad aimed at? Extending the idea of connotation beyond the words themselves, what is the effect of the unorthodox capitalization? Of the sentence fragments? Of the punctuation?

> #### the "IN" shop
>
> It's new, kitty cat! and it's crammed with goodies for lively young fashion buffs who think about style, think small about size, know pure pizzaz when they see it!
>
> Skitter down and go wild about the wow separates, the dresses and all!

What is the connection between the title and the language of the ad? Which words carry connotation for you? Which words could be considered fad words, the jargon of a special group? What group of buyers is the ad designed to stimulate? Can you find dictionary definitions for *buff*, *pizzaz*, *goodies*, *wow* (as an adjective), and *separates* (as a noun)?

4.   Winston Churchill, in discussing the formulation of code names for important military operations, suggested that names such as

"Massacre," "Jumble," "Bunnyhug," or "Ballyhoo" not be used. Instead he recommended that proper names selected from among those of heroes of antiquity, figures from Greek and Roman mythology, the constellations and stars, famous racehorses, and British and American war heroes be used. Why?

5. The synonyms in the following groups carry different connotations, although their denotations are roughly similar. Can you detect any differences in their meanings? Which would you most like to have applied to you? Which would you least like? Pick out any three sets of words and make up sentences illustrating their different shades of meanings.

   a. fastidious, fussy, particular.
   b. critical, fault-finding, picky.
   c. adventurous, foolhardy, rash.
   d. dull, stolid, impassive.
   e. story, lie, prevarication.
   f. take, steal, liberate.
   g. runty, petite, little.
   h. fad, vogue, style.
   i. cunning, artful, sly.
   j. unstable, fickle, capricious.

6. Do the italicized words in these sentences carry any connotation? Explain what it might be for each.

   a. He's really a card, *ain't* he? *He don't* care what he does just *so's* he gets a laugh.
   b. Does my baby *snookums doggy* want to bite the *dreat* big man?
   c He's *cool, man.* He beats the *craziest skins* in town.
   d. He's a real *gutty* fighter.
   e. Follow the *action* crowd—drink Sparkle Up!

7. What do you call the person of the opposite gender whom you like to socialize with? Sometimes young people complain that there is no term that they feel comfortable using, perhaps because of connotation. Which of these terms would you use? Which would you not use? Why?

   date   steady   girl (or boy) friend   sweetheart

8. Discuss the connotation implicit in each of these terms:

flatfoot   lawman   cop   policeman   officer   fuzz

Which of these are listed and defined in the dictionary? Does the dictionary discuss the connotation of any of them?

9. Using the dictionary if you need to, discuss both the denotation and the connotation of the following words. Remember, the connotation will perhaps vary from person to person. Whatever extra meaning a word suggests to any individual is its connotation for that individual.

founding fathers	Communist	vacation	draft
America	juvenile	marriage	democracy

3. Meaning and Context

If each word had only one meaning and that meaning were the same in all sentences, we might be able to understand one another better. But a typical word does not have just *a* meaning; it has a cluster of meanings. They have been acquired through the lifetime of the word and are often related in some way to a core of meaning basic to the origin of the word.

Each of these senses of the word is appropriately used in certain contexts. *Context* means the total environment in which the word appears; when we speak of context, however, we most often mean the *sentence context,* because this is where a word normally acquires its meaning. As a word appears in a sentence it interacts with other words and acquires part of its meaning from them. We cannot give the word *round* a single, precise meaning, for instance, until we see the word operating in sentence context: "He had only one round left in the firing chamber."

Consider the uses to which you would put the word *check* in each of these situations:

1. Paying bills.
2. Watching a basketball game or hockey match.
3. Playing chess.
4. Signing up for a room in a hotel.
5. Reviewing a column of figures to find an error.
6. Buying a fabric with a design marked off in small squares.
7. Paying someone to hang up your coat while at a dance.

Since most words have more than one sense, it is foolish to talk about word meanings without paying attention to the ways in which words are used in particular sentences. Yet we have all done this at one time or another and have blamed the dictionary for giving us poor information. The first definition listed by one dictionary for *tenderloin,* "the tenderest part of a loin of beef or pork," has little meaning for one who meets the word in this context: "He was a poor boy who rose above his low beginnings in the Tenderloin." One must read further in the dictionary entry for a sense which fits the context, in this case "a district in New York City in which there was much vice and corruption."

The best way to find the particular meaning you want in the dictionary is first to bear well in mind the context (whether sentence or paragraph) in which the word appears; second, to read carefully all the definitions listed for the word; and finally, to choose the definition which most nearly fits your context.

Which is the most appropriate definition for *dialogue* in the context which follows?

Context: The secretary of state flew overseas and carried on a high-level *dialogue* with the Israeli minister of foreign affairs.

Definitions: 1. A written work in the form of a conversation. 2. A talking together; conversation. 3. The passages of talk in a play. 4. An exchange of ideas or opinions.

But what if the meaning which you need in order to understand a particular word is not listed in the dictionary? Words, as you know, acquire new meanings as time goes by. Sometimes a new meaning, like a Broadway show, catches on suddenly and becomes a real smash. The meaning will be so new and its popularity so sudden that it will not appear in any but the most recent dictionary, and perhaps not even in that. A case in point is the verb *escalate,* which at the time of this writing is getting a big play in newspapers and magazines. It has become a fad word, and no story about international tensions can do without it. It appears frequently in sentences like these:

War talk escalated in the nation's capital as tensions heightened in Vietnam.

The chances of a steel strike are escalating as labor and management officials fail to reach an agreement.

> The president fears that another wage increase will escalate the cost
> of living to a new high.

The closest that most present dictionaries come to approaching this meaning is in the entry for *escalator,* a trade-name coinage, defined as "a moving staircase," and in the entry for *escalade,* which is "the act of scaling a fortified wall with ladders." These give us an idea, but, in the final analysis, we must rely on the clues furnished by the use of the word in sentence context in order to determine its meaning.

The first and second sentences hint that *escalate* means "enlarging" or "increasing" in some way. The third sentence hits the target more nearly, with the key word *high* suggesting the idea of "going up." These clues tie in neatly with the meaning we know for *escalator,* "moving staircase," and show the relationship between the two words. We acquire the sense of many words in just this way— by playing detective, consciously or unconsciously, and finding clues within sentences.

It is not true to say that context always gives an indication of a word's meaning. The sentence "He was a Babbitt type" does not tell much about the meaning of *Babbitt.* Likewise, the headline "Leaders of the World Eulogize Schweitzer" may suggest that *eulogize* means vaguely "something good," but only if you know who Dr. Schweitzer was. More often than not, though, context will give at least a general idea of a word's sense. We can reason easily, for example, that *folderol* means "something troublesome" in this context: "Can't figure out any other reason why a man should go through all the folderol of getting married." When we meet words often enough in varying situations, we will eventually close in on their specific meanings.

Reading experts tell us that we need not take a haphazard approach to finding meaning in context, that instead we can be looking for definite contextual patterns which appear in many sentences. Here are their most important suggestions:

1. Look for the restatement of an unknown word in the context which follows it. The restatement may be made by a known word or by an accompanying phrase, clause, or sentence.

> He was in a mood of complete *euphoria,* his happiness being the result
> of an announcement that he had won the sweepstakes.

Their greatest fear was of a *conflagration*, since fire would destroy their flimsy wooden settlement before help could arrive.

He was striving for a complete immersion into *mysticism*, the supreme religious experience.

He died *intestate*. In the absence of a will his property was divided among his heirs according to the laws of the state.

2. Look for contrasting words or statements which may help explain the unknown word.

The border incidents, which were uncommon and small a year ago, have now *proliferated* into daily, large-scale skirmishes.

One of the major dangers facing the country was economic collapse. As the fighting on all fronts reached its peak, the economy neared its *nadir*.

3. Look for key words which help limit the possible meanings of an unknown word.

The Indian government, being in an unusually *affable* mood, gave orders that he was to be civilly treated and hospitably entertained. (Which words help explain what *affable* means?)

In an effort to *placate* angry opponents and doubtful fence-sitters, Peking will introduce a softer line, perhaps even come out for a policy of "coexistence." (Which words clue you in on the meaning of *placate*? In what way does the thought of the whole sentence contribute to the word's meaning?)

If sentence context does not tell anything about a word's meaning, take a close look at the word itself. Here are two more suggestions. They ask you to consider the structure of the word.

4. Memorize the most common roots and affixes which help form so many English words. Then put your knowledge to work by analyzing the meanings of the component parts.

The tool, which directed water under high pressure through a narrow, pointed nozzle, was good for *subirrigation*. (What does *sub-* mean?)

The astronauts had to correct a number of minor *malfunctions*. (What does *mal-* mean?)

Copernicus believed in a *heliocentric* universe, rather than in the *geocentric* theory. (What do *helio-* and *geo-* mean? *Centric* suggests center.)

5. Look for a shorter word which you know inside a long, unfamiliar word.

> Since time *immemorial* the custom has been observed. (What word do
> do you recognize in this?)
> The *configuration* of the building *conformed* to that of a hexagon.
> (What words do you recognize?)

Exercises

1. Can context provide meaning for a nonsense word? A nonword, *trafopeder*, has been made up and inserted into the following paragraph. Read the passage and try then to write a definition for the verb "to trafopede."

> Among the most interesting "birds" you will ever meet on the road is the red-faced trafopeder. Let a horn blow behind him while he is driving and he starts trafopeding, his one response to a challenge from the rear. Does the motorist who is tailing him want him to give way and take a slower lane? The trafopeder's foot leaves the accelerator, compression takes over, and the car slows. Does an impatient driver behind him tootle the horn as a reminder that the traffic signal light has changed from red to green? The trafopeder moves his vehicle with infinite deliberateness, timing his crawl so that the tootler is trapped in the intersection while the light turns red once again. Trafopedic tactics may be emotionally satisfying to the trafopeder, but they are a dangerous frustration to the rest of the driving public.

2. Make up a word of your own; decide ahead of time what meaning it will have, and use it in a similar paragraph of your own creation. Make sure that context helps reveal the meaning of your word.
3. Bring to class a current newspaper or magazine. In class try to find three words from it which are unknown to you. After examining the complete context in which the words appear, even the paragraph if necessary, try to write definitions for the words. Then compare your definitions with those in a dictionary. It will be interesting to note how many contexts provide clues and how many will not. Copy the dictionary definitions listed for those words which have no contextual clues provided.
4. The following words have developed more than one meaning, or sense, throughout their life. Choose one word from the group and

read its dictionary entry, noting each of the separate senses. Then write an illustrative sentence for at least five meanings of the word, being sure to include the word in each illustrative sentence.

draft   round   square   charge   degree

5. As you know, many familiar words have different meanings when they appear in different contexts. Here are some sentences illustrating this fact. For each contextual example try to find a dictionary definition which corresponds to its meaning.

a. He'll have a fit if you don't *humor* him.
b. I have a sense of *humor,* but I just don't think it's funny.
c. You are certainly in a terrible *humor* today.
d. His *humors* are out of balance. That's why he is melancholy.

e. The *panel* was called to appear in Judge Long's court at 9 A.M.
f. He traded in his pickup for a *panel* delivery.
g. I am going to *panel* the wall in Philippine mahogany.

h. If you will bring over your T.V. set, I'll *fix* it for you.
i. When the radio signal comes on again, I'll take a *fix* on our position.
j. What a *fix* I'm in!
k. He was indicted for trying to *fix* a traffic ticket.
l. The drug addict was desperate for a *fix.*

m. I have a major in math but a *minor* in science.
n. *Minors* are not permitted in this establishment.
o. It was such a *minor* matter that I did not report it.

p. It didn't cost much—two dollars and a few *odd* cents.
q. After counting off, those with *odd* numbers take one step forward.
r. The dessert left an *odd* taste in my mouth.
s. I wish that I could find a mate for the *odd* shoe.

t. They are adding another *stage* to the rocket.
u. He is a star of *stage,* screen, and television.
v. At this *stage* of the game, Denver is ahead.
w. We will *stage* the next track meet in June.

x. May I look at the pictures in that *magazine?*
y. A well-placed bomb destroyed the whole *magazine.*
z. He put in a new *magazine* and the gun was ready for action.

6. Test yourself on the ability to determine word meanings from context. The following statements were taken from newspaper stories. Read them and look for clues within the sentences as to the meanings of the italicized words. Check your guesses with the dictionary.

   a. Two hundred dead Indians were counted on the battlefield after an *abortive* thrust against Jassar, northeast of Lahore.

   b. A remnant of this *coyness* remains in the unwritten rule that an active candidate must not show himself at the convention.

   c. *Surfeited* with too many speeches and red-eyed for lack of sleep, they may swear that this is their last convention.

   d. I have always held the view that these matters should be *bilaterally* settled between the parties directly involved— Pakistan and India.

   e. Violence did not *assuage* the hate that burned in Watts; it burns still.

   f. The march from Selma gave an *impetus* to the federal voting rights law.

   g. Unable to win a majority, both parties limped along, sharing the leadership of the *coalition* government.

   h. Using his Harvard-given *pseudonym*, he passed among them unknown.

   i. Although the man had been dead for two years, his book was published *posthumously*.

   j. People have tended to use the word as an *epithet* to describe anything distasteful.

   k. The mailman was leaving a free cake of soap at every mailbox, as part of the day's junk mail and as part of a big popular introduction for a new achievement in *saponification*.

   l. "Sonny's Blues" is the tale of two brothers, their *estrangement* and their painful reconciliation with each other.

SPECIAL PROJECTS

One way for you to increase your vocabulary is to become interested in and alert to unfamiliar words. You should provide many opportunities for yourself to experience them—either through direct involvement with their referents or through reading. The more you read, the more unfamiliar words you will discover in context.

Eventually, you will make them your own. Another way, a slower one, is to systematically assign yourself a new word to learn every day from the dictionary. Why not try it for a week? Pick out a word each day, copy the definitions, make up illustrative sentences for each of them on a card and glance at them several times a day. Most important, try to sneak the word into your conversation or writing at least once during the day.

5

Changes in Word Meanings

1. Inconstant Words

Anyone who has had difficulty reading and understanding Shakespeare's *Hamlet* (and everybody does) will agree that word meanings can change. When Hamlet, resolving to remember and avenge his father's murder, says, "Yea from the *table* of my memory I'll wipe away all trivial *fond* records," he is using *table* in its earlier sense of "a tablet" and *fond* in its earlier meaning of "foolish." Likewise, when Hamlet's mother, terrified and distracted by his strange behavior, is struck with amazement and "admiration," she is struck with wonder, not with approval or esteem. And when Hamlet goes to see his mother in her *closet*, he does not go to see her in a tiny room where her clothes are stored but in her bedchamber.

Examples such as these can be found on nearly every page of a Shakespeare play. To the dramatist and his contemporaries *ecstasy* meant "madness" rather more than it did "extreme rapture or happiness"; *conceit* meant "something that was imagined, an image, an idea," not "an exaggerated opinion of one's own abilities"; and *humor* called to mind several ideas—moisture, body fluids, and temperament—but not our common meaning, "that which is designed to be comical or amusing."

Such changes in word meanings have been taking place since the beginning of language, are occurring at the present time, and will be happening in the future. They are a part of the natural development of language. No one yet has been able to systematize all the ways by which these changes take place—they are uncertain and unpredictable—but a few interesting patterns have been noted.

Some words go through a long history with very little change; they mean approximately what they meant at their origin or have added only a few additional senses through the years. Other words progress through a remarkable series of transformations, alternately broadening and narrowing in meaning and ending with a sense which seems to have no relationship to the original referent. Still other words retain their basic core of meaning but add many additional senses, all relating in a clearly discernible way to the original idea. The ways in which these and other meaning changes occur will be discussed in the sections which follow.

2. Generalization of Meaning

Generalization is the name given to the widening of meaning which some words undergo. It implies a relaxing of specific meaning to include a broader, and often less definite, concept. A current example of this process is the word *fabulous,* which began with the meaning of "resembling a fable" or "based on a fable." Later it came to mean "incredible" or "marvelous," since the incredible and the marvelous were often found in fables. Nowadays the word is weakening in specific meaning still more. It has become a fad word, an adjective applied with little judgment or restraint to anything from a dress to a date. As you may have noticed, the specific meanings of *incredible* and *marvelous* are fading out in the same way. These words, too, are becoming weak expressions of approval.

A further example is the word *awful.* From a specific meaning of "inspiring awe," as in a phrase like "the awful majesty of God," it has generalized to mean "anything disagreeable or objectionable"— and even to function as a vague intensifier, as in "awful chance." As often happens with words like these, the original sense has disappeared almost completely.

Another interesting relaxation of meaning has occurred with words relating to time. *Presently, soon,* and *by and by* were understood in Shakespeare's time to mean specifically "at once," "immediately." Human nature being what it is, we can understand why the meaning of these expressions should have changed; what does *immediately* mean to a small boy when we tell him to put away his toys? Perhaps *immediately* will mean "pretty soon" to all of us, someday.

If we examine the etymologies of many words we will find that a good share of them have widened their meanings considerably. *Barn,* a compound of *bere* ("barley") and *ærn* ("place"), originally meant "a place for storing barley." Now a barn is a place where many things are stored. Both *assassin* and *thug* were at first names for members of Eastern religious sects who were dedicated to murder. Today these names refer to murderers and criminals of all kinds.

Examples can be multiplied: *brim* once meant only "water's edge"; *paper* for a long time was only "a sheet manufactured from the papyrus"; a *religious* person was only "one who had taken holy vows"; a *box* was only "a receptacle made out of boxwood"; and *manufacturing* was only "making by hand."

We have certain words which have generalized to such a degree that they can mean almost anything. *Thing,* for example, meant "a public assembly" or "a council" in Anglo-Saxon times. What does it mean now? You name it. *Article,* which has a number of specific meanings, is now acquiring, in addition, a meaning as vague as that of *thing. Business,* on the other hand, started out as a most general term, meaning literally "busy ness" or "that which keeps you busy." It then gathered several specialized meanings—but now seems to be coming full circle, as its area of meaning widens to include any vague referent, as in the sentence "This business disturbs me."

As we shall see later, the development of a word's meanings may often follow such a pattern of alternate specialization and generalization.

Exercises

1. Check the following words in your dictionary and write sentences explaining how each has generalized in meaning. (If the dictionary does not help, you will have to rely on your own observations of current word usage.)

proposition   place   situation   matter

2. Can you explain or illustrate how the following words are fading in meaning through overuse?

fantastic   terrible   great   tremendous

3. Look up the following words in your dictionary, read all the meanings carefully, and list those which you think have generalized.

picture   manuscript   hectic   scene

3.   Specialization of Meaning

When a word meaning specializes, it narrows to acquire a more specific meaning than it formerly had. The process is the opposite of generalization and occurs much more frequently. If you should read the prologue to Chaucer's *Canterbury Tales,* written in the late fourteenth century, you will encounter several words, now specialized, which then still had their generalized meanings. Here they are with their Middle English spellings and definitions:

licour: Any liquid.
fowles: Any bird.
mete: Any food.
flesh: Any meat.
starf: To die by any means.
deer: Any animal.
aventure (adventure):   Chance, luck.

Each of these, of course, has since come to mean something more specific.

A search through etymologies will reveal other examples of words which have narrowed in meaning since their early days. *Barbarian* was originally a vague designation for a foreigner of any kind; *garage,* when it was borrowed from France, meant "a place for storage." In the United States *lumber* has specialized to mean "timber or sawed logs especially prepared for use," but in Britain the word still retains its more general meaning of "unused articles," which are stored, incidentally, in a *lumber room. Disease* originally meant what its separate parts imply, *dis ease,* and referred to any kind of discomfort. The expression "to give up the ghost" and the biblical reference to the Holy Ghost may be the only remnants of an earlier, more general meaning for *ghost,* which once meant "spirit" or "breath." Now *ghost* has specialized to mean "a specter or apparition" of some kind. Perhaps the most startling specialization has taken place with the word *girl;* even as late as Chaucer's time it was used to mean "a young person of either sex."

Why do words specialize in meaning? Several theories have been suggested. It may be that when more than one word exists in a language to express the same idea, there is a tendency for one of the words to specialize in meaning. As we have noted, the word *starve* meant "to perish" in Middle English. But early in the Middle English period a new word was introduced for the same idea, the word *die*. As it became popular, it tended to replace *starve*, which began to specialize to mean "die of hunger."

Another theory to explain the narrowing of words is that as society changes, one aspect of a general meaning surges to the fore, becomes more important than the rest of the meaning. This theory might explain the specialization of the word *doctor*. Originally, the title *doctor* was given to one who was skilled in any learned profession. It is still bestowed on those scholars who have met certain scholastic requirements, but to many people in the United States, *doctor* means only the man of medicine, the man who becomes of some importance to them when they are ill. They may have little contact with an academic doctor, the Ph.D. For them the title has specialized to a noun synonymous with *physician*.

Exercises

1. Consult your dictionary and be ready to show that each of these words narrowed in meaning from an earlier, broader sense:

undertaker	wedlock	affection	corn
doom	corpse	science	virtuoso

2. Human beings tend to acquire many special names for things or ideas that are important to their cultures. Arabs, for example, are said to have hundreds of words for *camel*. They have separate words for milk camel, riding camel, freight camel, for pregnant camels, and so on. A Siberian tribe on the shores of the Arctic have about thirty words for caribou skins, caribou being their main source of food. Does this same idea hold true for us? How many special names, excluding brand names, can you list for *automobile?* For *doctor?* Can you think of other areas of our life whose importance is reflected by many special names? (How many names for *snow* do skiers know, for instance?)

4.   Elevation of Meaning

It is a curious fact that words can improve in reputation. Some words early in their history signify something quite low or humble, but change as time goes by to designate something elevated. For example, early in its history *angel* meant simply "a messenger," *marshall* and *constable* meant "a keeper of horses," and *governor* meant "a steersman, a pilot."

It is interesting to trace such rises in prestige. *Halo* for instance, once meant "a threshing floor on which oxen tread a circular path." From this meaning the idea of "a circle" was extracted and applied to the ring of light that seems to encircle the sun or moon. This application in turn must have suggested its application to a ring of light around the head of a saint.

No one today would object to being called *shrewd* or *nimble*, yet meanings of these words were at one time highly derogatory. A *shrewd* person was thought to be "wicked or rascally," and a *nimble* one to be good at taking things without permission. Two other words which are ameliorating, or rising, in reputation are *naughty* and *mischief*. As they were understood in Shakespeare's time, the former meant "wicked, bad, or evil" and the latter meant "serious harm, damage, or injury." Now, of course, we confine them largely to the mildly distressing deeds of small children.

One way to live down a derogatory name which has been attached to you is to make it a symbol of respect. This happened with two religious denominations, the Quakers and the Methodists. *Quaker* was a derisive name given by its critics to a religious group. It arose, reportedly, from the admonition of their leader, George Fox, to "quake at the name of the Lord." Although the early Quakers never did recognize this name (they have always called themselves the Society of Friends), the earlier implications of scorn have been lost. The term *Methodist* was contemptuously applied to John Wesley and his followers by fellow undergraduates at Oxford because of the methodical habits in study and in religious life that Wesley advocated. In time, of course, the name lost all its early suggestion of ridicule.

Exercises

Look up the following words in the dictionary and determine how they have risen in meaning. You may have to turn to the unabridged dictionary, in some cases.

Yankee	Whig	Puritan	minister
bachelor	nice	paradise	smart

5. Degradation of Meaning

It is much more common for word meanings to change in denotation from neutral to derogatory than it is for them to go the other way. This tendency, the opposite of elevation, is called *degradation* or *pejoration* of meaning. We can see pejoration taking place most clearly as we examine the words which were names for the common people in the Middle Ages. The word *vulgar* was then a colorless adjective for everyone not fortunate enough to be born into the upper classes of society. It meant literally "relating to the common people." It now has a primary meaning of "coarse, crude, boorish." *Homely* originally meant only "pertaining to the home in any way." Since homes were most simple, unpretentious, even plain, plainness became associated with the word. From "plain" it was just a step to "ugly" and transference of the word to people as well as the home. A *knave* was at first a servant, usually a young boy. The word later generalized to mean "a man of humble birth or status," and finally "a dishonest or deceitful person."

The words which named the workers on the farm coasted downhill as well. A *villain* was a farm servant in feudal times, not a wicked character. A *boor* was merely a peasant. Naturally, his manners and habits lacked refinement, so the word acquired the meaning of "a rude, awkward, ill-mannered person." Even today, the words *peasant* and *farmer* can be used in the same insulting way if one wishes to preserve the fiction that city people are vastly superior in refinement to country people.

Adjectives seem particularly susceptible to degradation. *Notorious* and *egregious* have declined from meaning "well known or outstanding in a good way" to meaning "well known or outstanding in a bad way." *Silly* changed from "good, blessed, and innocent" to "foolish," and *smug* changed from "neat, spruce, trim" to "self-satisfied and complacent." An *officious* person formerly was admired for doing his job well. Now he is criticized for "being too forward in doing his job."

Is there a human weakness revealed in this pejorative tendency? Would we rather be critical than otherwise? Or is it rather that the most powerful connotations—those that eventually change the denotation of a word—are the unpleasant ones?

Exercises

Consult your dictionary, the unabridged dictionary if necessary, and be ready to discuss the degradation in meanings of the following words:

mistress	hussy	wench
indifferent	artful	pedant
propaganda	pious	suggestive

6. Euphemisms

So far in this chapter we have been speaking of how the same word acquires different meanings. Now we will reverse the procedure for a moment and see how the same meaning can acquire a different word. It is very human to want to avoid discussing unpleasant things; yet some unpleasant topics are unavoidable. We cannot get away from them. In order to soften their impact, we have therefore adopted pleasanter words for them. We call such words *euphemisms*. Borrowed from the Greek, *euphemism* means literally "sounding good."

One of the topics which many people find painful to discuss is death. The word and other words connected with it carry connotations which may arouse severe emotional reactions, especially when someone very close has died. Consequently, we have a group of euphemisms which are employed when dealing with death and burial. We speak of people having "passed away" or of "passing on" or of being "deceased." Newspapers similarly speak of "fatalities" or "mortalities," perhaps because the Latinate words sound less personal. Establishments whose business is that of preparing bodies for burial and conducting funerals have actively promoted euphemisms. The *undertaker*, who was originally an "undertaker of funerals," is now a *funeral director* or *mortician*, even a *funeral counselor*. The *coffin* is now commonly called a *casket*, and graves are *plots* or *last resting places*. *Graveyards* are now less bluntly known as *cemeteries* or *memorial gardens*.

Euphemisms flourish in many areas of our life. It is likely that the phrase *juvenile delinquent* began as a substitute for a harsher term. Today we also have widely used euphemisms for the poor— the *underprivileged* and the *culturally deprived*.

Words which refer in any way to human anatomy or clothing often give way to euphemism. In Victorian days, when people were less frank than they were earlier or are now, *limbs* was substituted for *legs*. Likewise *breeches* came to be considered too crude for sensitive people to say, and it bowed to *pantaloons*, which was in turn replaced by *trousers*. *Pants*, a derivative of *pantaloons*, is still with us, though, so it may be that this madness has run its course.

In the world of occupations, jobs are often upgraded euphemistically. Car salesmen are publicized as "car counselors." We have engineers of every kind, from sanitary to custodial, and in at least one school system the people hired to assist with book rooms and audiovisual aids are called "para-professionals," a more impressive title than clerk.

Euphemism owes its usefulness to the effect of connotation. Some words sound better than others because they carry associations which create a desirable impression. In education, the trend is evident. High schools fortunate enough to have rugs on the floor in areas like the library or recreation room are careful to call them "accoustical floor coverings" in order to soothe the taxpayers. Standard colleges call themselves "universities"; schools of barbering, beauty, and business call themselves "colleges"; and schools which teach mechanical trades call themselves "institutes of technology." The yellow pages of the phone book can reveal some extreme examples; in one city are listed a Supermarket College, an Executive College of Barbering, a University Business College, and a Business Institute College.

Another kind of euphemism occurs when we substitute a milder term for an oath. *Goldarnit, egad, deuce* (for *devil*), *blessed* (when the opposite is meant), and *blooming* are all in this category. Such substitution for epithets was old in Shakespeare's time, when expressions like *zounds* ("by God's wounds"), *marry* ("I swear by Mary"), *'Sblood* ("by God's blood"), and *drot it* (a corruption of "May God rot it!") were common. H. L. Mencken, in *The American Language*, lists fourteen euphemisms for *damned: all-fired, blamed, blasted, blowed, confounded, darned, dashed, cursed, cussed, danged, deuced, dinged, switched,* and *swiggered.*

In a way, euphemisms are rather futile. They wear out quickly and must be replaced by other euphemisms. Still, there are times when they are useful. We can relieve our feelings harmlessly by uttering verbal substitutes for forbidden words; and in moments when we are emotionally vulnerable and sensitive, euphemisms can soften some of the harsh realities of existence, as in the case of death.

Exercises

1. What blunter terms do these euphemisms replace?

prevarication	perspiration	intestinal fortitude
urban renewal	attendance officer	mentally unsound
ecdysiast	inebriated	senior citizens

2. What happens to the words which are borrowed as euphemisms? Do their reputations change? How? Consider that *crazy* and *insane* were, at first, milder terms for *mad*. Also consider whether it is less offensive to be called a "juvenile delinquent" than to be called a "young punk"?

3. Can you think of any other euphemisms besides those mentioned in these pages? Make a list.

7. Proliferation of Meanings

As you can quickly verify by looking at the dictionary entries for *go, point, run, machine, wheel, gas,* or *pipe,* some words accumulate many meanings. The word *proliferation* might be used to describe one process which makes this accumulation of meanings possible. In one dictionary, *proliferation* is defined as "to grow by rapid production of new parts, cells, buds, or offspring" and applies primarily to the production of new parts by living organisms. But it can logically be extended to apply to words as well, since many words begin with one basic meaning and develop "bud" meanings as time goes by. All these "offspring" of the primary, early sense of the word relate logically to it:

The word *face* is a good example. Appearing for the first time in Middle English, it came without any change in meaning through Old French from an earlier Latin word, *facies* ("the face"). The first meanings of *face* in English was the most common and literal one: "the front of the head from the top of the forehead to the bottom of the chin, and from ear to ear." No argument there. But look at what other senses have come from this one. The first meaning has proliferated through processes of specialization, generalization, and metaphor into some remarkably diverse concepts, a few of which do not refer to the human anatomy at all.

Specialization has given us the senses of "an expression on the face" and "a distortion of facial expression." Through generalization of meaning we also can use *face* to stand for "one's whole outward appearance or attitude," as in the expression, "He put a good face on the matter." And since we must all assume the responsibilities for our actions as we *face* the world, the word has metaphorically come to assume the meaning of "reputation" as well. This sense, as in the expression "to lose face," we may have borrowed from the Chinese.

Again through generalization and metaphor, we have made *face* come to stand for "the surface of anything," whether it be the surface of a table, a cliff, or a banknote. Why? Perhaps because the human face is the surface which meets the world. From this sense a specialized meaning developed—"a marked surface, such as the *face* of a clock." (Remember our earlier discussion of dead metaphors?) Another narrowing sense is that which designates *face* as "any surface specially prepared, as of fabric, leather, etc." And finally, we have a generalized meaning, "the functional side of an object," as in the "*face* of a chisel."

The dictionary indicates that *face* is used in some interesting expressions as well: We can "face down" people, "face up" to a situation, have a "face to face" confrontation, "fly in the face of" danger, "pull a long face," "put a bold face on," and "set our faces against" someone.

Here is a diagram showing some of the senses of the noun *face* and their relationship to the original meaning (center) and to each other.

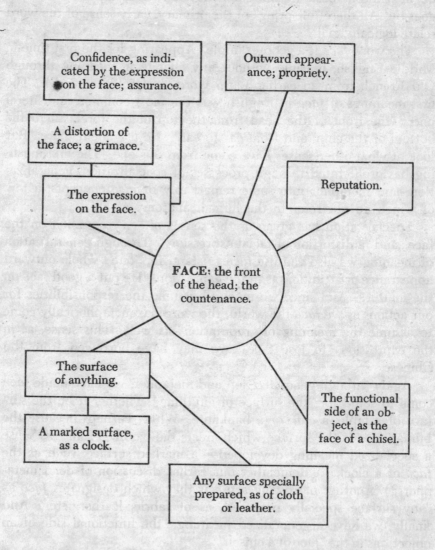

Some words develop meanings in such a way that it is difficult to imagine how one meaning can relate to another. The word *court* is a case in point. What does "a yard or courtyard" have in common with "to seek to attract by attentions and flatteries"? These are both useful and current meanings for the word; both meanings came from the same root; yet there is no immediately apparent common denominator of meaning to show a relationship. Why? The reason is that as the senses of *court* evolved, each succeeding meaning modified to some extent the idea of the preceding one. Eventually, some of the senses moved so far away from the early ones that no shadow of a connection is immediately evident to us.

In order to understand this process, we have to play detective, using the dictionary as our book of clues, carefully following the definitions as they are presented in chronological order, and making some educated guesses about them. Let us use *court* as an example. This word appeared in Middle English after the Norman conquest and thus was apparently borrowed from the French, who, in turn, received it from the older Latin word *cortis*, meaning variously "garden, poultry-yard, or enclosure." Another form of this Latin word is *cohortis*, which meant, in addition to the above definition, "a company of soldiers." Since we now have the word *cohort* in English, it appears that both it and *court* are cognates or *doublets*. Doublets are words which have different meanings but which were derived from the same source.

The *Oxford English Dictionary* indicates that *court*, when borrowed into English from the Old French, had already come to mean "the king's residence," the place where the king and his retinue "held state." Apparently, the word had extended some of its meanings in French even before it entered English. But whether the early development was in French or in English, the order of development seems clear. From the earliest meaning of "an enclosed area or yard," it came to refer to a space enclosed by walls or surrounded by buildings, and eventually to the buildings themselves, whether they were a manor house or the residence of the king himself.

The concept of buildings enclosing a space was borrowed also to apply *court* to "a quadrangular space opening off a street and built around with houses," such as we find in towns. We still find this idea current in our terms *court apartments* and *motor court*. From this sense, the "quadrangular space" part of the meaning was extracted, and *court* came to name any smooth quadrangular area upon which certain games were played—tennis originally, but now basketball as well.

How did *court* arrive at the meaning of "a court of law"? To find the answer we must go back to the meaning which designated a court as "the king's residence." In successive stages other senses were added to this. *Court* became not only the residence but also the people who lived there and the political function they performed. The king "held court", an activity which included both holding formal receptions of state for ambassadors and the like and dispensing justice, another of the king's duties. Eventually, the king designated officers to do this latter job for him, and *court* specialized to mean "the place where cases of law are heard" and "the session which occurs there."

Another major sense of the word grew out of the kind of life which was carried on in the king's residence. The *courtiers* ("members of the court") were expected to conduct themselves according to a code (*courtesy*) which, at its best, embraced notions of honor and chivalry. More commonly, however, *courtesy* referred to the elaborate manners of the court, such as the various terms which were used in addressing the king, his chief courtiers, and those of equal rank. Often, in the intrigue of court life, one had to use not only a "courteous" manner and speech, but flattery as well, in order to gain position or preferment. From this social-political aspect of court life we received phrases such as "to pay court to" and "to court favor," which the dictionary defines as "to seek to attract by attentions and flattery." Nowadays when we "go courting," we are looking for a marriage partner. The king's court, which gave rise even to this last sense, has all but disappeared, but the word *court* lives on through modern applications. Such extension and transfer of meaning is the way by which many words continue their usefulness. The dictionary, if we but learn to read it correctly, can make this point very clear to us.

Exercises

1. Turning to the dictionary etymologies of *face* and *facade*, explain why *facade* is a doublet, or cognate, for *face*.
2. Using the same procedure, explain why these sets are doublets:

coy and quiet	legal and loyal	card and chart
bugle and cow	bug and big	muscle and mouse
string and strain	guard and ward	regal and royal

3. Write a composition about the history of a word. Explain where the word came from, what its cognates may be, and how its meanings developed. Consult several dictionaries for information, including specialized dictionaries such as dictionaries of slang, dictionaries of American English, and the *Oxford English Dictionary*, if available in your public library. You will also want to consult the unabridged dictionary in your school library. A likely word to investigate is *board*, whose dictionary entry is reproduced at the end of Chapter 6. Other words which you may want to investigate are those which have been in the language a long while and are commonly used, words like *head, pipe, draw, tap, bill, bolt, flat, boot, point, check, line, scene, mark, square,* and *staff*. The best way to select a word to write about is to browse through the dictionary until you find one which looks interesting.

4. Although the first meaning of a word often relates directly and logically to all the other subsequent senses of the word, it does not necessarily follow that the first meaning is the "true" meaning and that the later meanings are inferior to it. As we have seen, meanings change with the demands of society, and early meanings often prove to be outmoded. The "true" meanings of any word are those which fit the needs of appropriate contexts. If the "true" meaning were the original sense of a word, and no other, the only correct response to the sound of the curfew would be to "cover your fire." And a credenza would be used only to receive dishes of food suspected of being poisonous. The words in the following list have modern meanings different from the literal original senses. Look them up in the dictionary and explain the connection between the earliest meaning and the modern meaning for each word.

calculate	candidate	bonfire
snob	bank	camera
slogan	pioneer	eavesdropping
earmark	marquee	carnival

Bibliography

The following books were useful in compiling the information in this chapter. They are also recommended to the student who wishes further reading.

Bryant, Margaret. *Modern English and Its Heritage*. New York: The Macmillan Company, 1949.

Greenough, James Bradstreet, and George Lyman Kittredge. *Words and Their Ways in English Speech*. Boston: Beacon Press, Inc., 1962.

Mencken, H. L. *The American Language*, abridged by Raven I. McDavid, Jr., with the assistance of David W. Maurer. New York: Alfred A. Knopf, Inc., 1963.

Robertson, Stuart, and Frederic G. Cassidy. *The Development of Modern English*, second edition. Englewood Cliffs, N.J.: Prentice-Hall, Inc., 1954.

6

The Development of the Dictionary

1. Glosses and Hard Word Books

Old dictionaries are fascinating. Some libraries have them tucked away in their stacks and you can check them out for examination: antique volumes with yellowed, musty-smelling pages, quaint-looking print, strange spelling, and fancy title leaves. Holding an early dictionary—the seventeenth century *Glossographia* by Thomas Blount, *An Universal Etymological Dictionary* by Nathaniel Bailey, or the folio volumes by Samuel Johnson and Noah Webster—is like holding history in your hand. It reminds you of other times, when dictionaries were written by individuals willing to spend a large part of their lives wrestling singlehanded with the language, rather than by committees of editors and scores of readers and secretaries.

They were intelligent, obstinate, even eccentric men, these lexicographers, as dictionary makers are called. As you read the prefaces to their word books, their personalities emerge. They express strong opinions about what should be in a good dictionary (theirs) and what is found in a bad dictionary (their competitors'). In their entries they often chat conversationally with the reader, let him know what they think of a certain word or author. They may define outrageous words which never saw anything but the most limited use (*circumbilivagination*, "going around in circles"). They may cheerfully confess that they have no idea of where a certain

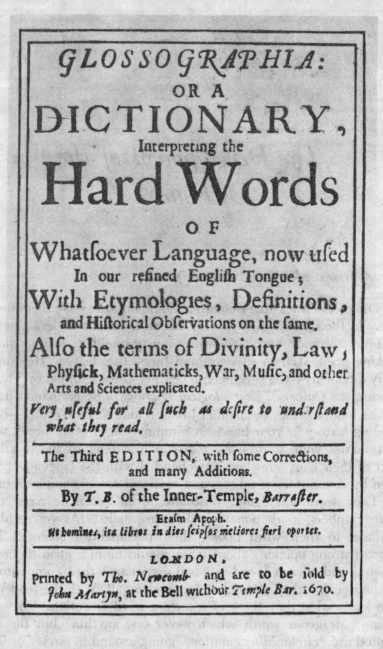

GLOSSOGRAPHIA:

OR A

DICTIONARY,

Interpreting the

Hard Words

OF

Whatſoever Language, now uſed
In our refined Engliſh Tongue;

With Etymologies, Definitions,
and Hiſtorical Obſervations on the ſame.

Alſo the terms of Divinity, Law,
Phyſick, Mathematicks, War, Muſic, and other
Arts and Sciences explicated.

*Very uſeful for all ſuch as deſire to underſtand
what they read.*

The Third EDITION, with ſome Corrections,
and many Additions.

By *T. B.* of the Inner-Temple, *Barraſter.*

Eraſm Apoph.
Ut homines, ita libros in dies ſeipſos meliores fieri oportet.

LONDON,

Printed by *Tho. Newcomb* and are to be ſold by
John Martyn, at the Bell without *Temple Bar.* 1670.

Title page from *Glossographia*, written by Thomas Blount.

word came from, and then hazard a guess. They may use an interesting story or joke as a verbal illustration for a word's meaning, as Johnson did in his entry for *rabbit*:

> **ra'bbit:** A furry animal that lives on plants, and burrows in the ground.
>
> "A company of scholars, going to catch conies, carried one with them which had not much wit, and gave in charge, that if he saw any, he should be silent for fear of scaring of them; but he no sooner espied a company of *rabbits*, but he cried aloud, *ecce multi cuniculi;* which he no sooner said, but the conies ran to their burrows; and he being checked by them for it, answered, who would have thought that the *rabbits* understood Latin?" —Bacon's *Apophthegms.*

Then, too, these early lexicographers may innocently present "scientific" information such as the following: "*Scolopendra*, a fish which feeling himself taken with the hook, casteth out his bowels, and then having loosed the hook, swalloweth them again." Modern dictionaries give us much more accurate information about the language, but the early ones were more charming.

Today, of course, none of these old dictionaries is in use. They have long ago been replaced by more complete, up-to-date, and accurate books. And so it goes; no dictionary lasts very long. Each gives way to an improved, usually larger book—but each new dictionary is built, in part, upon the efforts of earlier lexicographers.

And even though it inevitably lags behind, the dictionary's development has followed the growth of the language. As the language grows the dictionary grows. In its earliest stage the dictionary was nothing more than a brief list of translations for a few difficult words. Today the latest unabridged dictionary contains over 450,000 entries and can tell you more about a word than you probably care to know.

The forerunners of our modern dictionary appeared long ago in medieval England as the work of nameless scholars, poring over Latin manuscripts. As they read, they wrote in the margins easier Latin or English synonyms for some of the more difficult Latin words on the page, just as some students do today when they translate passages from a foreign language. Later, for the sake of convenience these words and definitions were collected into lists called *glosses*. In turn, several glosses were combined into a book called a *glossarium,* which was, in effect, a short Latin-English or English-Latin dictionary of selected words. The first English-Latin dictionary was printed in England in 1449. It had a Latin title, *Promptorium Parvulorum,* which means "A Storehouse for young boys."

It may seem strange that the first dictionaries in England were half Latin. But the truth is that Latin at this time was the international language of scholars, who considered it a more refined and important language than English. Latin carried the weight and prestige of the centuries. It was also the language of the church, the most important institution of the Middle Ages.

In the next century, as the international language of Latin began to lose ground and as foreign trade became more important to England, the glossarium reflected the changing times. It came to resemble our modern English–foreign language dictionaries, listing usually the English word first. An English-Welsh, an English-Italian, and an English-French word book were printed in the sixteenth century.

In the seventeenth century, with printing well established, the first real English dictionaries of importance appeared. They defined English words in terms of other English words, and in this respect resembled our dictionaries of today. They were different in other respects. For one thing, they defined only what the English called "hard words." The reasoning for this practice was very simple: Everyone knew what easy, everyday words meant; therefore, a dictionary to be useful should deal only with the words people were not likely to know. An additional justification for concentrating on hard words was that there were at that time more hard words coming into the language than an educated man might reasonably be expected to know. It appeared for a while that scholars were trying to convert English into a hybrid language composed mainly of Latin, with Greek and French words thrown in for good measure.

These early dictionaries were different from ours in another way, also. They gave very little information about a word, and what was given might very well be wrong. The definitions, which were often too short to be of any value, were the complete word entry. Of course, we must realize that these were books written by amateurs, mostly schoolmasters working in their spare time, dealing with an English language which had never received much scholarly attention.

Among the first English dictionaries published were Robert Cawdrey's *Table Alphabeticall of Hard Words* (1604), John Bollokar's *An English Expositor* (1616), and Henry Cockeram's *The English Dictionarie* (1623). Cockeram's book was the first in English to use the word *dictionary* in the title.

Nowadays a word has to be used to some degree in writing or speech before it is listed in a dictionary. A seventeenth century lexicographer did not give this restriction much thought. If he liked a word, in it went. Some words in the older dictionaries were merely Latin words which had been given a slight "face lifting" to change their appearance. It is easy to tell that these lexicographers borrowed extensively from previous Latin-English dictionaries.

The word lists had several divisions—a hard word section and sections made up of special categories of words, such as those found in mythology or law or science. Later on, more encyclopedic material was added, mostly geographical and biographical information. One early dictionary, Elisha Coles's *An English Dictionary* (1685), had a special section which listed and defined some of the jargon of the criminal underworld. He justified its inclusion in this way: "Tis no disparagement to understand the Canting Terms. It may chance to save your throat from being cut, or your pocket from being pickt." Modern editors also include slang terms in their dictionaries, but for a less practical and more scientific reason.

About half of the words in the old dictionaries have disappeared from our vocabulary. We do not run into words like *fallaciloquence* ("deceitful speech") or *pseudology* ("a false speaking out"). And we now have easier words for "fellow student" than *condisciple*. Words like these are listed, if at all, only in the *Oxford English Dictionary*, our great historical lexicon. Other jawbreakers, which are still on record in a comprehensive book such as the old *Century Dictionary*, are *fatigate* ("to fatigue"), *obstupefact* ("to induce stupidity"), and *obtestate* ("to beseech"). One word, *incompossible* ("not possible together, not compatible"), sounds as though Jimmy Durante made it up.

Many others of the hard words are still with us and doing useful service. We have *encyclopedia, excursion, conspicuous, malignant, consolidate, parenthesis, lexicon,* and *ostracize,* to name only a very few.

How were all these hard words created? Sometimes a word would simply be borrowed into the language without any change, like *appendix.* Or a word might have its Latin ending cut off, as when *perpetuatus* became *perpetuate.* Many of the words dropped the old endings, but added new ones—*acrimonia* became *acrimony* and *externus* became *external,* for example.

Not all Englishmen approved of the hard words which were flooding English. Fearing that their native Anglo-Saxon words might be overwhelmed and disappear, they condemned Latinate words as "inkhorn terms" concocted by overenthusiastic pedants, scholars who had lost their perspective. A few of the hard word critics took an extreme position and refused to use any recent creations from Latin or Greek. They harked back to the pure days of the language, to the native word stock of Anglo-Saxon, and tried to use in their writing only those words which had been in the language a very long time. When they needed a new word they would make up their own Anglo-Saxon compound or revive words from a much earlier time. Words such as *doom, dapper,* and *don* came to us in this way. Others—*bellibone* ("a fair maid") and *wrizzled* ("wrinkled and shriveled")—were less successful.

Eventually, the fad for hard words died down and the dictionary, which had hitherto been a book of difficult and specialized words, expanded its purpose to become a systematic record of the language. Common words as well as hard words were to be defined, a new idea in dictionary making. The change occurred in the next century.

Exercises

1. The word *gloss* has had many meanings throughout its history. Among others, it has had these: "a tongue," "a language," "a difficult word to be explained," "an explanation of a difficult word," "a superficial or misleading explanation," "a list of difficult words and their meanings." Using your dictionary if necessary, explain in a paragraph how all these meanings are logically related.
2. Which of the foregoing meanings does our modern word *glossary* most nearly fit?

3. How might the invention of the printing press have helped English win popularity over Latin as a dominant literary language in England?

4. *Thesaurus, lexicon, table alphabetical,* and *expositor* are early names for dictionaries. Look up their meanings and explain how each can mean a dictionary.

5. John Wesley, a famous eighteenth century churchman, wrote a hard word dictionary published in 1764, long after a new kind of dictionary had replaced that type. In his preface he tells about his book and criticizes other dictionaries for their faults. Read the following excerpt and then be ready to discuss (a) his concept of hard words and (b) the kinds of words which should be excluded from a good dictionary, according to Wesley:

> To this end it contains, not a heap of Greek and Latin words, just tagged with English terminations: (for no good English writer, none but vain or senseless pedants, give these any place in their writings:) not a scroll of barbarous law expressions, which are neither Greek, Latin nor good English; not a crowd of technical terms, the meaning thereof is to be sought in books expressly wrote on the subjects to which they belong; not such English words as *and, of, but,* which stand so gravely in Mr. Bailey's, Pardon's and Martin's dictionaries: but "most of those hard words which are found in the best English writers."

6. In the seventeenth century, it was not thought necessary to define common, "easy" words. When they were, they were dismissed with a very few explanatory words. How do modern dictionaries treat words like *set, put, from, and, of,* and *run?* Are the entries lengthy or short? Why? Do such words appear to be relatively easy to define or relatively difficult? Why?

7. Many of the hard words which appeared in seventeenth century dictionaries were taken, definitions and all, from a Latin-English dictionary by Thomas Thomas. In the list that follows are some of the original Latin words as found in Thomas's book. Look each one up in your dictionary, and note what changes, if any, have been made in the form of the word in order to turn it into English.

alacritas	anathema	catalogus	labyrinthus
rumino	horizon	celebro	circumspectus
deduco	apocryphus	acrimonia	adulatio

Above is the frontispiece of *The New World of Words,* compiled by Edward Phillips and printed in London in 1720. Facing page, top, is the title page. Facing page, bottom, is a typical entry from *The New World of Words.* From the collection of Maureen Songer, Portland, Oregon.

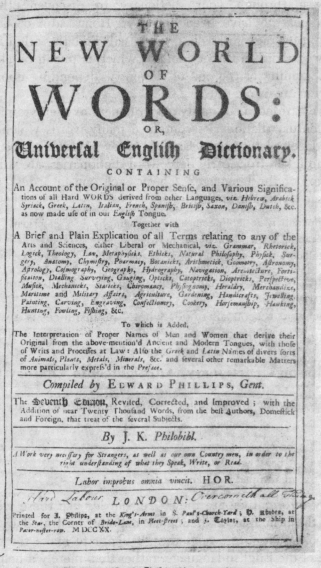

THE

NEW WORLD

OF

WORDS:

OR,

Universal English Dictionary.

CONTAINING

An Account of the Original or Proper Sense, and Various Significations of all Hard WORDS derived from other Languages, *viz. Hebrew, Arabick, Syriack, Greek, Latin, Italian, French, Spanish, British, Saxon, Danish, Dutch,* &c. as now made use of in our *English* Tongue.

Together with

A Brief and Plain Explication of all Terms relating to any of the Arts and Sciences, either Liberal or Mechanical, *viz. Grammar, Rhetorick, Logick, Theology, Law, Metaphysicks, Ethicks, Natural Philosophy, Physick, Surgery, Anatomy, Chymistry, Pharmacy, Botanicks, Arithmetick, Geometry, Astronomy, Astrology, Cosmography, Geography, Hydrography, Navigation, Architecture, Fortification, Dialling, Surveying, Gauging, Opticks, Catoptricks, Dioptricks, Perspective, Musick, Mechanicks, Staticks, Chiromancy, Physiognomy, Heraldry, Merchandize, Maritime* and *Military Affairs, Agriculture, Gardening, Handicrafts, Jewelling, Painting, Carving, Engraving, Confectionery, Cookery, Horsemanship, Hawking, Hunting, Fowling, Fishing,* &c.

To which is Added,

The Interpretation of Proper Names of Men and Women that derive their Original from the above-mention'd Ancient and Modern Tongues, with those of Writs and Processes at Law: Also the *Greek* and *Latin* Names of divers sorts of *Animals, Plants, Metals, Minerals,* &c. and several other remarkable Matters more particularly express'd in the *Preface.*

Compiled by EDWARD PHILLIPS, *Gent.*

The Seventh Edition, Revised, Corrected, and Improved ; with the Addition of near Twenty Thousand Words, from the best Authors, Domestick and Foreign, that treat of the several Subjects.

By J. K. *Philobibl.*

A Work very necessary for Strangers, as well as our own Country men, in order to the right understanding of what they Speak, Write, or Read.

Labor improbus omnia vincit. HOR.

Hard Labour LONDON: *Overcometh all Things*

Printed for J. Philips, at the *King's-Arms* in S. *Paul's-Church-Yard* ; D. Rhodes, at the *Star,* the Corner of *Bride-Lane,* in *Fleet-street* ; and J. Taylor, at the Ship in *Pater-noster-row.* MDCCXX.

Humores, *(Lat.* in *Physick)* Humours, of which three call'd general, wash the whole Body, *viz.* the Blood, the *Lympha,* a sort of pure Water, and the Nervous Juice. But there are several particular Humours, as *Chyle, Bile, Spittle, Pancreatick Juice, Seed, &c.* which see in their proper Places.

Humores Oculares, the Humours of the Eye, which are three in Number, *viz.* the *Aqueous,* or Watery, the *Crystalline,* or Icy, and the *Vitreous,* or Glassy ; which see.

8. Browse through your dictionary to discover other words which appear to have been borrowed from Latin or Greek with little or no change in spelling. You will find the original form of a borrowed word in the etymology, which is put in brackets either at the beginning or the end of the entry, depending upon the dictionary you are using.

9. Words are not necessarily as permanent as the pyramids; seventeenth century dictionaries contained many words which have disappeared completely from English today. Which of the following words, all taken from early hard word dictionaries, are still listed as being part of the language? Check each one in a desk dictionary first before trying the unabridged.

sesquipedalian	chironomer	cacography	emergent
deprecation	depredable	deprehend	advigilate
circumlocution	natation	neogamy	adolescenturiation

10. What reasons can you suggest for the disappearance of some of these words?

11. For what reasons or under what circumstances is a word likely to remain in the language?

2. Johnson's Dictionary, An Eighteenth Century Standard

The following are complete entries from a dictionary published in 1721:

cow: A beast well-known.

horse: A beast well-known.

dog: A quadruped, well-known.

Not very informative, are they? Yet entries like these were a step beyond the principle of dictionary making illustrated by the hard word books. They represented an attempt to make the dictionary a record of the English language, rather than merely a helpful guide to definitions of hard words. These entries came from *An Universal Etymological English Dictionary*, written by Nathaniel Bailey. One gets the idea that Bailey must have felt a little sheepish about presenting common word definitions, as if he expected to be told, "Any fool knows what a cow is!"

It was not Bailey but John Kersey who was the first to attempt a

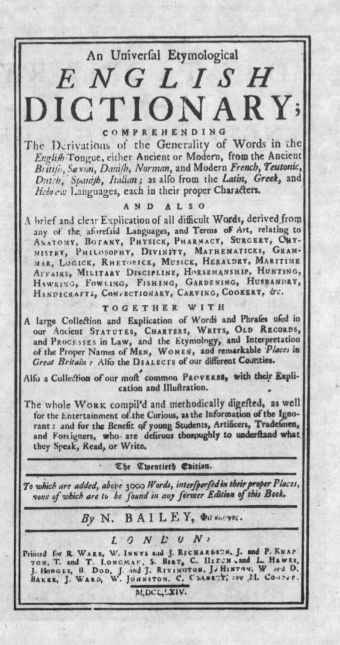

An Univerſal Etymological

ENGLISH
DICTIONARY;

COMPREHENDING

The Derivations of the Generality of Words in the *Engliſh* Tongue, either Ancient or Modern, from the Ancient *Britiſh, Saxon, Daniſh, Norman,* and Modern *French, Teutonic, Dutch, Spaniſh, Italian ;* as alſo from the *Latin, Greek,* and *Hebrew* Languages, each in their proper Characters.

AND ALSO

A brief and clear Explication of all difficult Words, derived from any of the aforeſaid Languages, and Terms of Art, relating to ANATOMY, BOTANY, PHYSICK, PHARMACY, SURGERY, CHYMISTRY, PHILOSOPHY, DIVINITY, MATHEMATICKS, GRAMMAR, LOGICK, RHETORICK, MUSICK, HERALDRY, MARITIME AFFAIRS, MILITARY DISCIPLINE, HORSEMANSHIP, HUNTING, HAWKING, FOWLING, FISHING, GARDENING, HUSBANDRY, HANDICRAFTS, CONFECTIONARY, CARVING, COOKERY, &c.

TOGETHER WITH

A large Collection and Explication of Words and Phraſes uſed in our Ancient STATUTES, CHARTERS, WRITS, OLD RECORDS, and PROCESSES in Law, and the Etymology, and Interpretation of the Proper Names of MEN, WOMEN, and remarkable *Places* in *Great Britain :* Alſo the DIALECTS of our different Counties.

Alſo a Collection of our moſt common PROVERBS, with their Explication and Illuſtration.

The whole WORK compil'd and methodically digeſted, as well for the Entertainment of the Curious, as the Information of the Ignorant : and for the Benefit of young Students, Artificers, Tradeſmen, and Foreigners, who are deſirous thoroughly to underſtand what they Speak, Read, or Write.

The Twentieth Edition.

To which are added, above 3000 Words, interſperſed in their proper Places, none of which are to be found in any former Edition of this Book.

By N. BAILEY, Φιλολογος.

LONDON:

Printed for R. WARE, W. INNYS and J. RICHARDSON, J. and P. KNAPTON, T. and T. LONGMAN, S. BIRT, C. HITCH and L. HAWES, J. HODGES, B. DOD, J. and J. RIVINGTON, J. HINTON, W. and D. BAKER, J. WARD, W. JOHNSTON, C. CORBETT, and M. COOPER.

M,DCC,LXIV.

Title page from Bailey's popular dictionary. This twentieth edition was published in 1764. Reproduced by courtesy of the Multnomah County Library, Portland, Oregon.

A

DICTIONARY

OF THE

ENGLISH LANGUAGE:

IN WHICH

The WORDS are deduced from their ORIGINALS,

AND

ILLUSTRATED in their DIFFERENT SIGNIFICATIONS

BY

EXAMPLES from the beſt WRITERS.

TO WHICH ARE PREFIXED,

A HISTORY of the LANGUAGE,

AND

An ENGLISH GRAMMAR.

By SAMUEL JOHNSON, A.M.

In TWO VOLUMES.

VOL. I.

THE SECOND EDITION.

Cum tabulis animum cenforis fumet honeſti :
Audebit quæcunque parum ſplendoris habebunt,
Et fine pondere erunt, et honore indigna ferentur.
Verba movere loco ; quamvis invita recedant,
Et verſentur adhuc intrâ penetralia Veſtæ :
Obſcurata diu populo bonus eruet, atque
Proferet in lucem ſpecioſa vocabula rerum,
Quæ priſcis memorata Catonibus atque Cethegis,
Nunc ſitus informis premit et deſerta vetuſtas.   Hor.

LONDON,

Printed by W. STRAHAN,

For J. and P. KNAPTON; T. and T. LONGMAN; C. HITCH and L. HAWES;
A. MILLAR; and R. and J. DODSLEY.

MDCCLV.

Title page from Dr. Samuel Johnson's dictionary of 1755. Reproduced by courtesy of the Multnomah County Library, Portland, Oregon.

universal dictionary of the language. Kersey is credited with producing several fine dictionaries between 1702 and 1708, all stressing the common word and aimed at the ordinary reader. He is also credited with producing the first unabridged dictionary. His innovations were noted and borrowed by Bailey, who compiled a dictionary of 950 pages and about 40,000 entries. Bailey's book was a great improvement over previous ones. He tried to draw his words from current usage; he occasionally discussed the etymology, or history, of the words (the information was often incorrect, however); he divided words into syllables; he tried to indicate correct pronunciation by marking the accent. In short, he put into his book many of the features of the modern dictionary. His dictionary served as a model for many to come.

Bailey's dictionary was followed twenty-one years later by one of the most successful of all early dictionaries. This was *A Dictionary of the English Language* written by Dr. Samuel Johnson, a critic and essayist considered by most of the artists and writers of his time to be the best judge and authority in matters of taste.

We know a great deal about Dr. Johnson because of his famous biography. Some witty and talented men of his time formed an exclusive but informal club with Dr. Johnson as leader. They gathered in London's Mitre Tavern for evenings of good talk, exchanging gossip and opinions about literature, politics, the theater, or anything else of interest. One man, James Boswell, so admired Johnson that he wangled his way into the club and spent as much time as possible in Johnson's company, taking notes on the things he did and the remarks he made. After Johnson's death Boswell published the results of his long association, *The Life of Samuel Johnson, L.L.D.*

When he first conceived the idea of making a standard dictionary, Johnson estimated that he could complete the task within three years. He missed the publication date by about five years. In 1755, eight years after he had signed the contract with his booksellers, Johnson's dictionary was published. Singlehanded, except for the aid of six copyists working in a converted loft, he had compiled a book almost 2,300 pages long—two and a half times as long as Bailey's. It was published in two volumes, each nine and one-half inches wide, fifteen and one-half inches long, and three and one-half inches thick. It contained about 40,000 entries, each developed with a completeness previously unmatched. From Boswell's biography we learn that writing the dictionary was not a happy experience for Johnson. He worked in near-poverty, was forced to draw all his commission in advance before the work was ever published, and was burdened with the illness of his wife much of the time. He expected to get additional financial support from Lord Chesterfield but was disappointed. Still, he persevered, and when the volumes were finally published they were hailed as a standard by which all dictionaries could be measured.

How did he accomplish this tremendous job? He drew upon his extensive background as a scholar and his experience with the

Portrait of Dr. Samuel Johnson by Joshua Reynolds.

language. He also had a good reference shelf to consult when necessary. His task was made easier because he used Nathaniel Bailey's dictionary as a starting point. In fact, we are told that he worked from an interleaved copy of Bailey's book, which means probably that he inserted blank sheets between the pages and made notes from Bailey's word list. In many cases he rejected Bailey's words. Some he took but expanded the definitions considerably. Plagiaristic? Perhaps. But the truth of the matter is that all dictionaries are built upon other dictionaries. Even modern editions are based upon revisions of previous materials, for the most part; it would be a Herculean task to start from scratch. Yet it seems only fair that Bailey should share some of the credit that has gone to Johnson as the creator of the first standard dictionary of the English language.

For nearly one hundred years after its publication Johnson's dictionary was *the* dictionary in England and in America. What were its merits? Although it was not the best dictionary in the world at that time (superior books were being created both in France and Italy by academies of scholars), this was the best dictionary created by a single man. Its outstanding features can be summarized as follows:

1. It was the most comprehensive dictionary of English.
2. It had extensive etymologies, or word histories.
3. The definitions generally were both complete and clear.
4. The various senses or meanings of the same word were numbered and distinguished.
5. Definitions were followed by quotations from reputable authors in order to illustrate the use of a word, thus adding another, most important dimension to definition. The entry for *horse*, for example, had six different verbal illustrations, including Shakespeare's famous "A horse! a horse! my kingdom for a horse."

Johnson's dictionary was by no means perfect, however. For one thing, there were errors. He defined pastern as "the knee of a horse," for instance, when actually it is part of the foot. When a woman later asked him how he came to make such an error, Johnson is said to have replied, "Ignorance, Madam, pure ignorance."

A few of his definitions were difficult to understand:

network: Anything reticulated or dessicated, with interstices between the intersections. [But how would *you* define it?][1]

cough: A convulsion of the lungs, vellicated by some sharp serosity.

He can also be criticized for allowing his personal prejudices to creep into his definitions, although they make interesting reading:

excise: A hateful tax levied upon commodities, and adjudged not by the common judges of property, but wretches hired by those to whom excise is paid. [Johnson's father once had trouble with the excise tax commission.]

pension: An allowance made to anyone without an equivalent. In England it is generally understood to mean pay given to a state hireling for treason to his country.

He defined the two political parties in England as follows:

tory: One who adheres to the ancient constitution of the state, and the apostolical hierarchy of the church of England, opposed to a whig.

whig: The name of a faction. [Which party do you think he belonged to?]

Johnson even had his little joke on himself:

lexicographer: A harmless drudge.

Unlike modern dictionaries, Johnson's had a personal tone. He made judgments and decisions, confessed frequently that he was not sure of an etymology or a meaning, and might even point out that one of the literary authorities he was quoting was in error. Notice these entries:

dogbolt: Of this word I know not the meaning, unless it be that when meal or flower is sifted or bolted to a certain degree, the coarser part is called dogbolt, or flower for dogs.

fraischeur: Freshness; coolness. A word foolishly innovated by Dryden.

job: (A low word now much in use of which I cannot tell the etymology.) . . . petty, piddling work; a piece of chance work.

dissever: (*dis* and *sever.*) The particle *dis* makes no change in the signification, and therefore the word, though suggested by great authorities, ought to be ejected from our language.

---

[1] From *Johnson's Dictionary: A Modern Selection*, by Samuel Johnson, edited by E. L. McAdam, Jr. and George Milne. © Copyright 1963 by E. L. McAdam, Jr. Reprinted by permission of Pantheon Books, A Division of Random House, Inc.

spick and span: (This word I should not have expected to have found authorized by a polite writer . . . a low word.) Quite new. Now first used.

writative: A word of Pope's coining; not to be imitated.
"Increase of years makes men more talkative, but less *writative;* to that degree, that I now write no letters but of plain how d'ye's." — Pope to Swift.

Although he perhaps disapproved of them, Johnson included a large number of what he called either cant or low words. We would call them jargon or slang. Most of Johnson's slang words, like our own, had a short life. How many of these have you ever heard?

kicksey-wicksey: A made word in disdain and ridicule of a wife.

dandiprat: A little fellow; a urchin; a word used sometimes in fondness, sometimes in contempt.

to conjobble: To settle, to discuss. A low cant word.

to prog: To rob; to steal; . . . a low word.

clodplate: A stupid fellow; a dolt; a thickscull.

to proctor: To manage. A cant word.

Johnson's dictionary had a number of Latinate words as well, a legacy from the hard word books and from some of the early authorities whom he relied upon. Do you need a word to describe the act of taking off your shoes? He had it—*discalceation.*

As the examples show, Samuel Johnson felt that he should make judgments about words and their use. The older hard word books merely defined words. The eighteenth century wanted more than definition; it wanted a standard, and Johnson tried to supply it. Along with other lexicographers of his time, he was aware of what he considered to be the defects in the language. He felt that in earlier times the language had reached a state of excellence, but that since then it had slid downhill. Foreign influences had crept in and it had been, as he put it, "exposed to the corruptions of ignorance and caprices of innovation."

What to do about it? Try to stop the downhill slide by compiling a dictionary which would be an authority on language. Choose words, make good judgments about their merits, and select illustrations for definition from the best English writers. With the authority of the standard dictionary as a guide, the language might be stabilized. As Johnson said in his lengthy preface, he and others hoped that his dictionary might "fix our language and put a stop to those alterations which time and chance have hither-to been suffered to make in it without opposition."

But by the time that he had finished writing his two volumes, he was convinced that the natural course of language change cannot be stopped. He continued in his preface to say that his reason and experience finally told him that a lexicographer is foolish who believes that "his dictionary can embalm his language, and secure it from corruption and decay. . . . sounds are too volatile and subtle for legal restraints; to enchain syllables, and to lash the wind, are equally the undertakings of pride." Time seems to have borne out Johnson's view of linguistic change. The language continues to go its merry way: words die, new ones are born, "barbarities" flourish.

Exercises

1. When Johnson wrote that his dictionary might "fix our language," he did not use *fix* in the common sense, meaning "to repair or to mend." Look in your dictionary, scan the listed definitions for *fix*, and choose the one which seems to fit Johnson's context.

2. Johnson said about the word *dissever*: "The particle *dis* makes no change in the signification, and therefore the word, though suggested by great authorities, ought to be ejected from our language." Look up *dissever* and the prefix *dis-* in your dictionary and provide an explanation of this apparent inconsistency. (What is the real function of *dis-* in this instance?) Assuming that Johnson is all for logic in words and definitions, what might he object to regarding the definitions attached to the word *scan*?

3. Do you agree with him about the word *dissever*? Can you think of any other word like this which has the same meaning with or without its prefix?

4. Using your dictionary, check these words from Johnson's dictionary and list those which have survived to this day: *dogbolt, fraischeur, job, dissever, spick and span, writative, kicksey-wicksey, dandiprat, conjobble, prog, clodpate, proctor, discalceation.*

5. Is there any evidence from the few examples listed here and from Johnson's comments about them that a lexicographer's judgments about words have little to do with the paths that words may take in the future?

6. Imagine for a moment that you are Johnson, about to write your dictionary. Where, aside from a basic word list from another dictionary, would you find the words to admit to your book? What criteria would you use to admit or reject words? Would you let in words which you personally dislike? Would you feel it your duty to comment about the usage of the word? Where would you get your verbal illustrations? How would you treat a word if it has more than one meaning?

7. Without reference to a dictionary try writing definitions for *desk, pencil, cough,* and *network*. Which were the most difficult? Why?

SPECIAL PROJECTS

1. Boswell's life of Johnson is especially readable because it contains many interesting anecdotes about Dr. Johnson and members of his famous club and records some of his idiosyncrasies and witticisms. Browse through the book, make notes, and report to the class on those incidents and remarks that help reveal the kind of person he was.

2. In the same book find an account of Dr. Johnson's famous letter to Lord Chesterfield regarding the dictionary and the circumstances which prompted the letter. Report your findings to the class and read Dr. Johnson's letter to them.

3. Secure a copy from your school or local library of *Johnson's Dictionary: A Modern Selection*, edited by E. L. McAdam, Jr. and George Milne (Pantheon Books). Browse through it and report any interesting or unusual entries to the class.

3. Noah Webster and the American Dictionary

When Johnson died in 1784 a good American dictionary had yet to be written. There were many good dictionaries on the market, but they had all been created in England. Noah Webster, born in 1758, felt that what America needed was a good American dictionary. Strongly nationalistic (could you be eighteen years old in 1776 and not be?), Webster believed that he could improve on Dr. Johnson's two volumes and, at the same time, meet the special needs of American English. Like most of the early lexicographers, this schoolmaster-scholar criticized his predecessor's work. Perhaps this criticism was partly strategy, to convince the public that it needed a new dictionary. But in any event, Webster pointed out that Johnson's book was often inaccurate, contained many low, vulgar, and Latinate (hard) words, and displayed a poor selection of illustrative authorities. (Actually, many of Johnson's authorities were good, but the examples he chose were sometimes poor ones.) What we needed was a dictionary which would correct these errors and expand the word list to include American words and their special meanings.

Webster believed that our language was changing from that of the British because we were isolated geographically from them. New words, new meanings for old words, different pronunciations, and new usages were the results of the isolation. Why should America have to use a British dictionary which did not take any of these factors into account? Webster let it be known that he was the man to write the great American dictionary. And he did.

Following the publication of a small, five-thousand-word dictionary in 1806 and an abridgement of it in 1807, he spent the next twenty years, off and on, working on his great *An American Dictionary of the English Language*. Like Johnson's, this was a one-man dictionary. Webster wrote the manuscript in his own hand, all 70,000 entries. He was seventy years old when it was published in 1828. Imagine the work and the scholarship which went into it! There were literally years of learning other languages in order to become an expert in etymology, of tracing word origins, of formulating clear definitions, of weary reading in order to find apt verbal illustrations, of doing the million and one editorial tasks which must be performed before a dictionary is complete. The publication was an event of scholarship, and it deserved to be. But it received both good and bad reviews. Many people thought that it was an improvement over Johnson's dictionary and that at last America had the lexicon it deserved. Others thought that it was presumptuous of this Yankee spelling-book author to try to improve upon Johnson's work.

As the title promised, this was an American dictionary, and Webster emphasized the fact in several ways. His definitions pointed out differences between American and British usage and meaning. The dictionary included many words of American origin which did not appear in any British dictionary. Webster was also proud of the illustrative quotations of Americans which followed many of his definitions to help make the meaning of the word clear. Ben Franklin, George Washington, John Jay, Washington Irving, and other famous Americans took their place as authorities alongside Shakespeare, Milton, and the Bible.

Often when he had no quotation available he made up his own or used one from his earlier writings. These always had a strong religious, patriotic, or moral flavor, like the entry which follows:

> **indebted:** . . . We are indebted to our parents for their care of us in infancy and youth; we are indebted to God for life; we are indebted to the Christian religion for many of the advantages and much of the refinement of modern times.

Webster saw his dictionary as a moral guide as well as a reference book. Like the Bible, it should uplift the mind and inspire the soul with quotations. It should also teach patriotism through properly selected quotations. In his mind, it was not just a dictionary; it was an inspiring textbook. Unlike Johnson, he was not willing to admit many vulgar words into his dictionary.

Noah Webster should be remembered warmly by every child who ever had trouble with spelling, because he tried to simplify it. He believed, along with his friend Ben Franklin, that those people spell best who do not know how to spell. In short, words should be spelled just as they sound. He and Franklin even talked together about introducing a new phonetic alphabet, but nothing came of it. Webster did try, however, to introduce a simplified spelling for certain words. His guiding principle was to eliminate all silent letters in a word and to use only those letters whose sound would clearly follow the pronunciation.

Some of his spellings look strange: *bred* for *bread, masheen* for *machine, fether* for *feather, fantom* for *phantom, karacter* for *character,* and *iland* for *island.* Others look natural to us because they are now accepted: *honor* for *honour, music* for *musick, center* for *centre, theater* for *theatre, draft* for *draught,* and *ax* for *axe.* It took courage for Webster to try to change American spelling. The public was not willing to accept most of his reforms, and he was often made fun of in print. For example, jokers and critics would send letters to him or to newspapers which read like this:

Deer Mistur Webstur,

    I am a nacheral born speller, never tuk a lessun in my lif, and am just the man tu help yu with yur nu dikshunary, I wurk cheep.

Hiram Jonz

Attempts since the time of Webster to simplify spelling have met with similar resistance and few new spellings have arrived. Apparently we like words to appear just as we are used to seeing them.

Even though his dictionary of 1828 was a great achievement, it was not a financial success, partly because Webster's publisher had money troubles and partly because in the absence of a copyright law competitors were bringing out abridged volumes which sold for less than his twenty-dollar standard dictionary. Webster revised it in 1841 when he was past eighty, mortgaging his home to finance the revision. He did not live to see the day when his book became a standard item in every home, alongside his popular spelling book and the Bible. Its great popularity came later, after the rights had been sold to George and Charles Merriam and the book was revised once again. In 1847 the Merriam revision, which sold for six dollars, made the name of Webster a household word. The Merriam company has published Webster dictionaries ever since.

Incidentally, the name *Webster* is common property today. It is not restricted to Merriam dictionaries. It appears in the titles of many dictionaries put out by other publishers, whether such dictionaries be the drugstore paperback or the six-dollar hardback collegiate edition. Obviously, the name appears in these titles because it inspires confidence in the product. To some people *Webster* is a synonym for *dictionary*.

During Webster's time other good American dictionaries appeared. His chief American rival, Joseph Worcester, published dictionaries which battled for the market with the Merriam books until the time of the Civil War.

Critics today like to point out that in some respects Noah Webster has been overrated. Some claim that his rival, Worcester, made a better dictionary. They also tell us that Webster was not as good a scholar as he should have been, that the conclusions he came to about the origins of words were often wrong, that he ignored the new information about language origin and development which was available to him, that he was prejudiced against the upper classes of society and would not accept their pronunciation as a standard for his dictionary, and that, in general, he was a stubborn, cantankerous, opinionated man.

All agree, however, that in some respects he had talents which make a great lexicographer. He had the fortitude to see an epic task through to the end. He had the determination to carry out his beliefs regarding language in the face of criticism and adversity. Above all, he could write clear, concise, accurate definitions. As one later editor said of him, "He was a born definer of words."

Webster died in 1843. Since that time great American and British dictionaries have appeared with regularity. But they are the results of corporate efforts, the work of language specialists— etymologists, philologists, and the like—who are highly trained and who have at their fingertips the latest language findings of modern scholarship. With Webster's death the era of the one-man dictionary ended.

Exercises

1. The preface to *The Century Dictionary and Cyclopedia* (last published in 1914 and one of our great American dictionaries) has some interesting remarks about the function of a lexicographer. What might Noah Webster have to say about this one?

> Of the great body of words constituting the familiar language the spelling is determined by well-established usage. . . . it is not the office of a dictionary like this to propose improvements, or to adopt those which have been proposed and have not yet won some degree of acceptance and use.

2. What are your own opinions on this statement based upon your reading and discussion so far?

3. Do modern lexicographers agree with Webster that a dictionary editor has the responsibility of trying to improve the reader's attitudes toward God and country through the use of selected verbal illustrations?

4. Copy the quotation from the *Century* in question 1, simplifying the spelling by omitting all letter *e*'s which are silent. When you are through, consider these questions: Would a system like this

make spelling easier? How does it look to you? What other specific spelling simplifications can you suggest?

5.   What problems would be encountered if a simplified spelling system were adopted?

6.   Webster once stated that American English will in time be "as different from the future language of England as the Modern Dutch, Danish, and Swedish are from the German, or from one another." Obviously, he was wrong. What influence do you think that the increased travel between England and the United States and the interchange of British and American films and T.V. programs have had upon the languages of both countries?

4.   Since Webster's Time

Although they present their word information in about the same way, dictionaries since Webster's time have become larger and more accurate. They are smaller in bulk, but a typical modern desk dictionary contains about twice as many entries as did Webster's dictionary of 1828. This physical compression is possible because thinner paper and smaller type are used. And whereas Webster (and earlier lexicographers as well) seemed to use a "by guess and by golly" approach to etymology, today's editors draw upon a well-established body of accurate information. They know beyond much doubt about the ancestry of English and its related family languages and can tell you in most cases where a word came from.

Today there are many good commercial dictionaries for sale. What many people consider to be among the best dictionaries ever published is no longer printed. This was the *Century Dictionary*, first published in 1891, last published in 1914. Containing 450,000 entries, it compared in size and excellence to our most modern unabridged dictionary. The *Century* made an impressive desk set with its ten volumes in sturdy, textured brown bindings embossed with gold lettering. One of the volumes was a cyclopedia of proper names; another was an atlas. The editor, William Dwight Whitney, was a noted scholar who produced a book admired for its completeness, its excellent hand-set typography, and its admirable treatment of words. If you ever visit used-book stores with an eye to snapping cheat¹ (chet), *v.* [< ME. *cheten*, confiscate, seize as an escheat, a clipped form of *escheten*, escheat: see *escheat*, *v.* and *n.*, and cf. *cheat*¹, *n.* The sense of 'defraud,' which does not occur until the latter part of the 16th century, arose from the unscrupulous actions of the *escheaters*, the officers appointed to look after escheats: see *escheator*, *cheater*.] **I.** *trans.* **1†.** To confiscate; escheat.

Chetyn, confiscor, fisco.   *Prompt. Parv.*, p. 73.

2. To deceive and defraud; impose upon; trick: followed by *of* or *out of* before the thing of which one is defrauded.

> A sorcerer that by his cunning hath *cheated* me
> *Of* the island.   *Shak.*, Tempest, iii. 2.

> To thee, dear schoolboy, whom my lay
> Has *cheated of* thy hour of play,
> Light task, and merry holiday !
>   *Scott*, Marmion, L'Envoi.

Another is *cheating* the sick *of* a few last gasps, as he sits
To pestle a poison'd poison behind his crimson lights.
        Tennyson, Maud, i. 11.

3. To mislead; deceive.

> Power to *cheat* the eye with blear illusion.
>   *Milton*, Comus, l. 155.

> All around
> Are dim uncertain shapes that *cheat* the sight.
>   *Bryant*, Journey of Life.

4. To elude or escape.

> A fancy pregnant with resource and scheme
> To *cheat* the sadness of a rainy day.
>   *Wordsworth*, Excursion, vii.

We an easier way to *cheat* our pains have found.
        M. Arnold, Empedocles on Etna.

5†. To win or acquire by cheating: as, to *cheat* an estate from one. *Cowley.*—**6.** To effect or accomplish by cheating: as, to *cheat* one's way through the world; to *cheat* one into a misplaced sympathy.

Selfishness finds out a satisfactory reason why it may do what it wills — collects and distorts, exaggerates and suppresses, so as ultimately to *cheat* itself into the desired conclusion.   *H. Spencer*, Social Statics, p. 179.

To cheat the gallows, to escape the punishment due to a capital crime; escape the gallows though deserving hanging.

The greatest thief that ever *cheated the gallows*. *Dickens*.

Syn. 2. To cozen, gull, chouse, fool, outwit, circumvent, beguile, dupe, inveigle.

II. *intrans.* To act dishonestly; practise fraud or trickery: as, he *cheats* at cards.

Entry from *The Century Dictionary and Cyclopedia*, edition of 1891. Note how our modern sense of *cheat* came about.

up bargains, watch for sets of this dictionary. For five or ten dollars you may become the owner of a treasure. Of course, for practical work the *Century* has one obvious disadvantage—it contains no words coined since the early 1900's. In 1927 a new, condensed version appeared called *The New Century Dictionary*.

Another noted turn-of-the-century dictionary was Funk and Wagnalls' *Standard Dictionary of the English Language,* first published in 1893. It emphasized spelling and pronunciation and introduced the practice of placing current meanings first in its definitions. Like the Merriam company, Funk and Wagnalls today produces a complete line, from an unabridged dictionary on down through desk and school dictionaries.

In a class by itself is a dictionary published by the Oxford University Press in England. This set, called first *A New English Dictionary on Historical Principles,* is the *Oxford English Dictionary.* It is the most complete dictionary of the English language in existence. Unlike the dictionaries you have been reading about in this chapter, the *OED,* as it is familiarly known, is not a commercial dictionary. It is a book made up by and for the use of scholars of the language. Its thirteen volumes sell for well over three hundred dollars, a little more than the average man wants to pay for a dictionary, so it is sold mostly to schools and libraries.

The *OED* is not a dictionary to which you turn to see whether or not a certain word is a "good" word to use. It is a book which attempts scientifically to record the history and development of every printed word in the language from the time of King Alfred (about A.D. 1000) to the current date of publication. Unlike Johnson's dictionary and others of that kind, the *OED* does not try to set a standard for English. It tells you as completely as possible what the language is and where it has been. Beginning with the earliest occurrence of each word, the *OED* furnishes the reader with dated quotations to illustrate the use of the word as it developed through time. At least one illustration of usage per century has been given for each word throughout its entire history, and frequently there are more. Its etymological information is almost overwhelming; even the various spellings each word has had in its lifetime are recorded.

The entries for single words in the *OED* often run on for pages. The word *set* with its definitions and other materials fills more than eighteen pages, *go* fills thirty-five columns, and over seventy separate senses are given for *get*.

In all, the *OED* contains over 414,000 definitions, which are, in turn, illustrated by almost two million quotations. The total number of words in all the volumes is estimated at fifty million.

In order to compile this massive collection of information about our language, the editors had to collect more than five million excerpts from English writings. The collecting of language samples began in 1858; the editing of the material started in 1878, twenty years later. In 1928, seventy years after the collecting started, the final volume came from the presses. With its historical perspective of English and its disclosure of the ways in which language operates, this dictionary has had a tremendous influence upon all succeeding lexicographical theory. If ever a work deserved the adjective *definitive*, this is it.

Incidentally, this concept of a "national" dictionary of a language is not exclusive to English. Work has been going on sporadically for thirty-eight years on a Scottish dictionary, which aims at giving a complete account of Scots words since the year 1700. The present editors hope to have it completed by 1976. Likewise, a group of scholars in Italy, the Crusca Academy, is editing a monumental dictionary of the Italian language. The aim of the Academy is to make a definitive record of Italian from about the year 1100.

Exercises

Here is the complete entry for *board* as found in *Glossographia*, a dictionary written by Thomas Blount and published in 1670. Examine it and the succeeding entries for *board* from later dictionaries, that are found on pages 130 and 131, and then answer the questions that follow.

BOARD [SAX] BERD Du]: a Plank, a Table.
To BOARD, to cover with BOARDS;
    to diet or entertain at TABLE;
    to be dieted, boarded.
To go ABOARD, to go into a Ship.
TO BOARD (Sea Term) is to draw nigh to a Ship during the night,
    in order to enter Men on any Part of her.
BOARD and Board (Sea Term) is when two Ships come so near as
    to touch one another.

This is the complete entry for *board* from Dr. Samuel Johnson's *Dictionary of the English Language* (1775). Reproduced by courtesy of the Multnomah County Library, Portland, Oregon.

¹board \'bō(ə)rd, -ȯ(ə)rd, -ōəd-ȯ(ə)d\ *n* -**s** [ME *bord* piece of sawed lumber, table, shield, ship's side, border, fr. OE; akin to OHG *bort* ship's side, ON *borth* piece of sawed lumber, table, Goth *fotubaurd* footstool, Skt *bardhaka, vardhaka,* adj., cutting off, *bardhaka, vardhaka,* n., carpenter, and perh. to Gk *perthein* to destroy] **1** *obs* **:** BORDER, SIDE, EDGE **2 a :** the side of a ship **b :** the stretch that a ship makes on one tack in beating to windward **:** TACK **3c 3 a :** a piece of sawed lumber of little thickness but considerable surface area usu. being rectangular and of a length greatly exceeding its width, in technical specifications of a thickness not exceeding 2½ inches and a width of from 6 to 12 inches, and designated according to thickness ⟨a half-inch ~⟩ ⟨a 2-inch ~⟩ — compare BATTEN; see *board* pl (1) **:** STAGE 2b(1) : STAGE 15c ⟨if intellectual ideas were to vanish from the ~ I am not sure that my heart would break —Max Beerbohm⟩ **c boards** *pl, slang* **:** SKIS **4 a** *archaic* **:** TABLE 3a (1) **b :** a table on which food is customarily served esp. when spread with a meal ⟨bade the fellow call help to clear the ~ where still was set their interrupted noontide meal —Rafael Sabatini⟩ ⟨a feast spread upon the ~⟩ **c :** food in the form of daily meals often provided as payment for services ⟨room and ~⟩ ⟨~ was the most expensive item in his budget⟩ ⟨the job gave him bed, ~, and 10 dollars a week to spend⟩ **d :** a table at which a council or the magistrates of a court sit ⟨sit as a guest at the council ~⟩ **e :** a number of persons appointed or elected to sit in council for the management or investigation of a public or private business, trust, or other organization or institution ⟨a ~ of advisers to the mayor⟩ ⟨~ of directors⟩ ⟨a university examining ~⟩ **f :** LEAGUE, ASSOCIATION ⟨the local ~ of underwriters⟩ **g :** an examination given by an examining board — often used in pl. ⟨passed his ~s⟩ **h** (1) **:** the exposed hands of all the players in a stud poker game (2) **:** an exposed dummy hand in bridge **5 a :** a flat usu. rectangular piece of material (as wood) often marked off or provided with pegs and used for some special purpose (as the playing of certain games or the providing of a flat or hard surface on which to cut food or set dishes) ⟨a gaming ~⟩ ⟨a molding ~⟩ — see BACKBOARD, SIDEBOARD, SPRINGBOARD, WARPING BOARD **b :** a wall or a specially constructed flat usu. rectangular device attached to a wall or free standing used for varied purposes (as the posting of notices, the listing of stock-market quotations, or the display of theater advertisements esp. where they may be seen by large groups or by the general public) ⟨stock quotation on the ~ of a brokerage house⟩ ⟨~d with playbills in front of a theater⟩ **c :** a panel (as of wood) on which electrical circuit components (as jack) are mounted **d :** PARI-MUTUEL MACHINE **e :** any of various forms used in finishing fabrics and knitted garments (as hosiery); see ²BOARD **8** I (1) ; a device that is used in bridge for holding the four hands of a deal in their original form so that they may be played more than once (as in duplicate bridge) and that consists usu. of a flat oblong container with four pockets for the hands dealt and is marked on its face to show which player is dealer and who is vulnerable — called also *tray* (2) ; the particular distribution of cards in duplicate bridge constituting any one deal as contained in such a board : a deal in duplicate whist or bridge (3) ; the entire process of bidding and playing such a deal (4) ; the score accruing to the winning side when such a deal is played; *esp* ; one match point (5) ; the greatest number of match points that can be scored on any deal in duplicate bridge **6 a :** any of various wood pulps or composition materials formed or pressed into somewhat stiff or rigid flat usu. rectangular sheets; *specif* ; material of the same general composition as paper but stiffer and usu. thicker, being in one classification at least ¹²⁄₁₀₀₀ inch thick — compare PAPER **b :** the stiff foundation piece for the side of a book cover ⟨bound in ~s⟩ ⟨~ binding⟩ **c :** PRESSING BOARD **7** *chiefly Austral* **a :** the part of a woolshed where sheep are sheared **b :** the sheep about to be sheared **c :** the crew of shearers **8 :** an organized exchange providing facilities for buying and selling securities or commodities **9 :** a fixed signal governing the movement of trains ⟨a slow ~⟩ ⟨a clear ~⟩ — **board on board** *or* **board and board** *or* **board by board** *archaic, of ships* **:** side by side **:** close beside each other — **go by the board** **1 :** to go or be carried by force over the side of a ship ⟨in the storm the masts *went by the board*⟩ **2 :** to go or be thrown into discard **:** be passed by and beyond recall — **on board** **:** ABOARD

²board \"\ *vb* -ED/-ING -s [ME *borden,* fr. *bord* piece of sawed lumber, table, shield, ship's side, border] *vt* **1** *archaic* **:** to come up against or alongside of (a ship) usu. for the purpose of attacking **2 :** ACCOST, ADDRESS ⟨he ~*ed* me with some light remark —W.A.White⟩ **3 a :** to go on board of or enter (a ship) **b :** ENTER ⟨~ a train⟩ ⟨~ an airplane⟩; MOUNT ⟨a motorcycle⟩ **4 :** to cover with boards or boarding ⟨store owners taped and ~*ed* their windows —*Springfield (Mass.) Daily News*⟩ — usu. used with *up* ⟨~*ing* up the windows of the empty house⟩ **5 a :** to provide with regular meals or with regular meals and lodging usu. for a compensation ⟨the question is, will she — as well as lodge her guest —Clara Morris⟩ ⟨~*ing* students⟩ **b :** to place where board or board and shelter or other accommodations are provided usu. for a compensation ⟨~ a horse at a livery stable⟩ **6 :** to haul (the tack of a course on a sailing vessel) down to the deck or to the bumpkin **7 :** to work or rub with a board ⟨as in graining leather⟩ **8 :** to shape (knitted garments) by processing on special forms ~ *vi* **1 :** TACK *vi* **1 :** to have one's regular meals or regular meals and lodging provided usu. for a compensation ⟨having ~*ed* for a time at the Rutledge Tavern —Ruth P. Randall⟩

This is the complete entry for *board* from *Webster's Third New International Dictionary,* edited by Philip B. Gove, copyright 1961 by G & C Merriam Company. Publishers of the Merriam-Webster Dictionaries.

1. You have just seen the entries for *board* as they appeared in three dictionaries: Thomas Blount's *Glossographia* (1670), Samuel Johnson's *A Dictionary of the English Language* (1755), and *Webster's Third New International Dictionary* (1961). Referring to the entries when necessary, answer these questions:

    a. What did the word *diet* apparently mean in Blount's time? Is this meaning still in existence? (Check in a modern dictionary to see.)

    b. Which dictionary relies most on verbal illustrations by famous authors?

    c. What reasons can you suggest for the more extensive etymology in the modern dictionary?

    d. In what particular ways is Johnson's entry different from Blount's?

    e. In what particular ways is the modern dictionary's entry different from Johnson's?

    f. Suggest some reasons why the modern dictionary has the most definitions and word derivatives for *board*.

2. Summarize your discussion of these questions by writing a paragraph about dictionary changes.

3. Reproduced on the opposite page is the entry for the adjective meanings of the word *dizzy* as it appears in the *OED*. Examine the entry carefully and try to find the answers to the following questions:

    a. How many numbered senses, or meanings, are listed?

    b. How was the word spelled in Old English (OE.)?

    c. What was the earliest meaning, now marked *dialectal*?

    d. How many verbal examples are given for meaning 4?

    e. Which meaning of *dizzy* do you think is now most common?

    f. What is the earliest date listed for any verbal illustration?

    g. What is the latest date listed for any verbal illustration?

    h. We have an informal use for the word *dizzy* nowadays, as in the expression "a dizzy blond." Which numbered definition would you fit this phrase under?

    i. We also have a modern context for *dizzy* in a sentence like "The car raced at a dizzy speed." Would you place this illustration under one of the listed definitions, or would you add a new meaning?

    j. How can you account for the change in meaning between sense 1 and senses 2 and 3?

Dizzy (di·zi), *a.* Forms: 1 dysiᵹ, dyseᵹ, 2-3 dysiᵹ, dusiᵹ, dusi(e (*ü*), 2-6 desi(e); 4-6 dyz(s)y, (6 dusey), 6-7 dis(s)ie, -y; 6-7 dis(s)ie, 7- **dizzy.** [OE. *dysig, dyseᵹ* foolish, stupid = OFris. *dusig*, MDu. *dosech, dösech*, LG. *dusig, dösig, dussig* giddy, OHG. *tusig, tusic* foolish, weak, a common WGer. adj. in *-ig* (-Y), from a root *dus-* found also in LG. *dusen* to be giddy, OE. *dyslic, dyselic* foolish, stupid, and in a different ablaut grade with long vowel in LG. *dûsel* giddiness, MDu. *dûzelen*, Du. *duizelen* to be giddy or stupid. See early ME. derivatives under DUSI-.]

1. Foolish, stupid. Now only *dial.* (Not in general use since 13th c.)

c825 *Vesp. Hymns* vii, Swe folc dysiᵹ. c950 *Lindisf. Gosp.* Matt. vii. 26 Gelic bið were dysᵹe se ðe ᵹetimberde hus his ofer sonde [c1160 *Hatton* desien men]. 971 *Blickl. Hom.* 41 Geþenc, þu dyseᵹa mon. c1175 *Lamb. Hom.* 117 Þer þe dusie mon bið þriste and þer þe dwolunge rixað. a1225 *Ancr. R.* 182 Nolde me tellen him alre monne dusiᵹest? a1250 *Owl & Night.* 1466 Dusi luve ne last noht longe. a1275 *Prov. Ælfred* 479 in O. E. Misc. 131 Wurþu neuere so wod, ne so desi of þi mod. 1876 *Whitby Gloss.*, *Dizzy*, half-witted. 1893 BARING-GOULD *Cheap Jack Z.* II. 45 Such dizzy-fools that they put their money there.

†b. *absol.* A foolish man, a fool. *Obs.*

c825 *Vesp. Psalter* xci. 6 Dysiᵹ ne onᵹiteð ða. c1175 *Lamb. Hom.* 33 Hwet seið þe dusie. *Ibid.* 105 Wreððe harð wununge on þes dusian bosme. a1225 *Leg. Kath.* 599 Ha ne stod neauer, ear þene þes dei, bute biforen dusie.

2. Having a sensation of whirling or vertigo in the head, with proneness to fall; giddy.

c1340 HAMPOLE *Pr. Consc.* 771 Than waxes his hert hard and hevy. And his heved feble and dysy. 1526 SKELTON *Magnyf.* 1052, I daunce up and down tyll I am dyssy. 1568 TURNER *Herbal* I. 20 [Wolfesbayne] maketh [men]dusey [ed. 1551 dosey] in the head. 1581 MULCASTER *Positions* xvi. (1887) 73 For feare they be disie when they daunce. 1653 H. COGAN tr. *Pinto's Trav.* xiii. 40 They were so exceeding dizzy in the head that they would fall down.

1852 MRS. CARLYLE *Lett.* II. 200 With my heart beating and my head quite dizzy. *fig.* 1726-46 THOMSON *Winter* 122 The reeling clouds. Stagger with dizzy poise, as doubting yet Which master to obey.

3. a. Mentally unsteady or in a whirl; **b.** Wanting moral stability, giddy.

1501 DOUGLAS *Pal. Hon.* Prol. 101 My desie heid quhome laik of brane gart vary. 1599 *Broughton's Lett.* ii. 9 Meere buzzings of your owne conceited dizzie braine. 1671 MILTON *P. R.* II. 420 At thy heels the dizzy multitude. 1780 COWPER *Table Talk* 607 He .. dizzy with delight, profaned the sacred wires. 1875 JOWETT *Plato* (ed. 2) I. 61 My head is dizzy with thinking of the argument. 1879 MISS JACKSON *Shropsh. Word-bk.*, *Duzzy*, stupid; confused. 'I'm mighty duzzy this morning.'

4. Accompanied with or producing giddiness.

1605 SHAKS. *Lear* IV. vi. 12 How fearefull And dizie 'tis, to cast ones eyes so low. 1643 MILTON *Divorce* Ded., Did not the distemper of their own stomachs affect them with a dizzy megrim. 1818 S. ROGERS *Columbus* I. 24 The very ship·bey on the dizzy mast. 1855 MACAULAY *Hist. Eng.* IV. 561 He began..to climb..towards that dizzy pinnacle.

5. Arising from or caused by giddiness; reeling.

1715-20 POPE *Iliad* v. 381 Lost in a dizzy mist the warriour lies. 1740 PITT *Æneid* XII. (R.), A dizzy mist of darkness swims around. 1781 COWPER *Hope* 518 The wretch, who once..sucked in dizzy madness with his draught. 1863 GEO. ELIOT *Romola* II. vii, Thought gave way to a dizzy horror, as if the earth were slipping away from under him.

6. *fig.* Whirling with mad rapidity.

1791 COWPER *Iliad* XXI. 10 Push'd down the sides of Xanthus, headlong plung'd, With dashing sound into his dizzy stream. 1795-1814 WORDSW. *Excursion* VIII. 179 The..stream, That turns the multitude of dizzy wheels

7. Dull of hearing. *dial.*

1879 MISS JACKSON *Shropsh. Word-bk.*, *Duzzy*, deafish. 'E's lother duzzy; e doesna 'ear very well.'

8. *Comb.*, as *dizzy-eyed, -headed.*

1591 SHAKS. *1 Hen. VI*, IV. vii. 11 Dizzie-ey'd Furie .. Suddenly made him from my side to start. 1611 COTGR. *Estourdi*, dulled, amazed .. dizzie-headed. 1654 TRAPP *Comm. Ps.* cvii. 33 A company of dizzy-headed men

From The *Oxford English Dictionary Being a Corrected Re-Issue of a New English Dictionary*, edited by James A. H. Murray, Henry Bradley, W. A. Craigie, and C. T. Onions. Reprinted by permission of The Clarendon Press, Oxford.

Bibliography

Baugh, Albert C. *A History of the English Language.* New York: Appleton-Century-Crofts, Inc., 1957.

Boswell, James. *The Life of Samuel Johnson*, abridged by Bergen Evans. New York: The Modern Library, 1952.

Laird, Charlton. "Language and the Dictionary," *Webster's New World Dictionary of the American Language*, Second College Edition. Cleveland: The World Publishing Company, 1970.

Laird, Charlton, and Robert M. Gorrell. *English as Language: Background, Development, Usage.* New York: Harcourt, Brace & World, Inc., 1961.

McAdam, E. L., Jr., and George Milne. *Johnson's Dictionary, A Modern Selection.* New York: Pantheon Books, 1963.

Mencken, H. L. *The American Language*, abridged by Raven I. McDavid, Jr., with the assistance of David W. Maurer. New York: Alfred A. Knopf, Inc., 1963.

Pyles, Thomas. *Words and Ways of American English*. New York: Random House, Inc., 1952.

Sledd, James A., and Gwin J. Kolb. *Dr. Johnson's Dictionary, Essays in the Biography of a Book*. Chicago: University of Chicago Press, 1955.

Starnes, DeWitt T., and Gertrude E. Noyes. *The English Dictionary from Cawdrey to Johnson, 1604–1755*. Chapel Hill, N.C.: The University of North Carolina Press, 1946.

Warfel, Harry R. *Noah Webster, Schoolmaster to America*. New York: The Macmillan Company, 1936.

Whitehall, Harold. "The Development of the English Dictionary," *Webster's New World Dictionary of the American Language,* college edition. Cleveland: The World Publishing Company, 1959.

7

Modern Dictionaries

1. General Dictionaries

Modern dictionary making is big business. Publishing companies invest large sums of money, employ staffs of scholars, and hire salesmen and advertising people to try to put their product on every school desk and in every home. Commercial dictionaries, in effect, blanket the market. They are found in paperback, hip-pocket size in supermarkets and drugstores, in specially edited elementary and high school volumes, and in the larger but still abridged volumes called *desk dictionaries*. A few publishers put out the ultimate in the commercial dictionary, the unabridged, sold mostly to schools, libraries, newspaper and magazine offices, and to individuals with a special need for a definitive volume. Commercial dictionaries range in price from fifty cents to fifty dollars and differ in quality and content to a tremendous degree.

Most of them are surprisingly good; in fact, America, which started late in the dictionary-making business, has exceeded England in providing good, versatile word books for the general public. It is still a good idea, however, to be knowledgeable about the quality, scope, and content of the dictionaries available.

2. Pocket Dictionaries

At their worst, the pocket dictionaries are little more than spelling lists with scanty, often inaccurate definitions. At their best they are 50,000-entry abridgments (shortened versions) of reputable desk dictionaries. Even these pocket dictionaries have certain disadvantages. They fall apart readily when given steady use; they lack adequate illustrations, contextual or otherwise; the print is eyestraining; they do not give sufficient entries or complete enough entries to satisfy anyone but the casual user; their etymologies are either missing or oversimplified.

They do have some advantages. They are cheap—everyone can own a dictionary which retails for less than a dollar—and they are portable. There is something to be said for a dictionary which can be carried from school to home and from class to class so easily. And the definitions in the reputable paperbacks are accurate, even though limited. For a student who needs a dictionary by his side to check a spelling or the meaning of an occasional word from his reading, a paperback is a good investment. For most other purposes paperback dictionaries are inadequate.

3. Desk Dictionaries

The most satisfactory dictionary for all-around use is the one-volume workhorse called the desk dictionary. Its title will identify it variously as a desk dictionary, a standard dictionary, a college dictionary, or a collegiate dictionary. Some contain the name *Webster* in their titles because of the reputation of Noah Webster, but the name itself is no guarantee of quality, since it is now in the public domain and any publisher may use it.

Many desk dictionaries are on the market, but the best ones are those published by well-known and reputable companies, who put their prestige on the line and throw their great resources into the making of a quality product. The making of a dictionary does not come cheap, but if a company can afford the long period of preparation, the financial rewards are usually worth it. Of all the dictionaries on the market, the "big five" are the following:

Name	Number of pages	Number of entries
American Heritage Dictionary	1,600	155,000
Random House Dictionary	1,600	155,000
Standard College Dictionary	1,632	150,000

Name	Number of pages	Number of entries
Webster's New World Dictionary	1,692	157,000
Webster's Seventh New Collegiate Dictionary	1,220	130,000

These books sell in the six- to nine-dollar range, some in hard covers, and are roughly about the same size. All are excellent dictionaries and are either new or recently and completely revised. The *Standard* and *Webster's Seventh* were redone in 1963; the *Random House* and *American Heritage* were brand new in 1967 and 1969 respectively; and *Webster's New World* (Second Edition) had its major revision in 1970. Desk dictionaries such as these carry much more information than most people imagine. In addition to word meanings, the reader can find maps; biographical data about famous people living and dead; rules of grammar, punctuation, and capitalization; forms of address; proofreader's marks; instructions on the preparation of manuscripts; tables of weights and measures and signs and symbols; a history of the alphabet; lists of colleges and universities in the United States and Canada; and the most concise, interesting, and authoritative information about the English language—origin, development, grammar, usage, dialects, spelling, and the like—to be found anywhere.

Although these dictionaries are similar in quality, they vary in small ways. Some assume more authority for designating "correct" usage than do others. *Webster's Seventh* makes a point of letting the reader know how the language *is* being used and is sparing with usage labels; by contrast, the *American Heritage Dictionary* employed a usage panel of 100 experts (mostly writers) to tell the reader how they think the language *should* be used. The panel's decisions are found in more than 800 usage items throughout the book. Several dictionaries are strong in the presenting of etymological information (word origins). *Webster's New World* and the *American Heritage* both give much attention to the Indo-European roots of English, so that the reader may, if interested, see how many English words descended from the 1500 root words in the parent language of English. The *American Heritage* is proud of its many illustrations (over 4000), made up of both line drawings and photographs.

Formats differ also. *Webster's Seventh* puts its gazeteer, biographical names, and other supplemental information in the back of the book. The rest, to varying degrees, incorporate this material into the main text in one single alphabetical order.

Webster's New World, utilizing the scholarship of Mitford M. Mathews, the leading authority on Americanisms, marks with a star all words which originated in America. This is also the only dictionary which comes with its own phonograph record—a recording of the pronunciation key, so that the reader can hear the sounds spoken as he reads the key in the book. The *American Heritage*, which is rather stuffy about usage, threw "conservatism" to the winds by including all the "four-letter" words within its pages. The editors of *Webster's New World*, on the other hand, explained that they chose to leave them all out of their new edition because "the terms in question are so well-known as to require no explanation."

On the following page are entries for the word *gargoyle* taken from leading desk dictionaries. Examine them and note that they all give the same essential information, they all have a picture of a gargoyle (do they all try to keep up with one another?), but that the entries vary in minor ways.

Someday you may want to buy your own desk dictionary. How can you tell which is the best to buy? You cannot rely heavily on the advertising claims for each, since the advertisements are written by advertising agencies who may make claims that are erroneous, overblown, or immaterial. For example, one reputable dictionary is touted in advertising as a "final word authority—relied upon by courts of law, schools and colleges, the United States Government Printing Office, and public libraries," but actually its editors assert that the book is to be thought of as the opposite of authoritarian. as a descriptive dictionary rather than one which tells infallibly about words and their use! The best way to evaluate dictionaries is simply to examine them with some criteria in mind. Here are points which you should consider.

1. *The date of the last major revision of the dictionary*. This information is important, since dictionaries should keep up with the changes in language, but revision dates may be difficult to determine. Dictionary publishers are reluctant to give out this information when it has been a long time since the last revision. Copyright dates are misleading in this regard; a new copyright date does not indicate that a substantial amount of new material has been added

o a dictionary. One way to tell how recently a book has been
horoughly worked over is to read the introduction or preface. If
he book has been revised lately, you can be sure that the publisher
vill inform you of the fact there. If it has not, the matter will not be
mentioned. Another way to check the currency of a dictionary is to
ook up a word of fairly recent origin, a word like *miniskirt* or the
lang term *acid*. Most reputable dictionaries are extensively revised
ibout every ten years, and in the meantime are updated when pos-
ible at each printing. Other things being equal, the book to buy is
he one with the newest materials in it.

gar·goyle (gär′goil), *n.* [ME.
gargulie; OFr. *gargouille;*
see GARGLE], 1. a waterspout,
usually in the form of an
elaborately carved animal or
fantastic creature, projecting
from the gutter of a building.
2. a projecting ornament (on
a building) like a gargoyle
in appearance.

GARGOYLE

(A)

gar·goyle (gär′goil)
n. A waterspout,
usually made in the
form of a grotesque
human or animal fig-
ure, projecting from
the gutter of a build-
ing. [< OF *gar-
gouille* throat]

GARGOYLES
a Cathedral of Amiens, 13th century.
b Cathedral of St. Eustache, Paris,
16th century. *c* Church of Mont-
martre, Paris, 19th century.
d Chrysler building, New York,
20th century.

(C)

gar·goyle (gär′goil), *n.* a spout,
often terminating in a grotesque
head (animal or human) with open
mouth, projecting from the gutter
of a building for carrying off rain
water. [ME *gargulye, t.* OF: m.
gargouille, gargoule, appar. the same
word as *gargouille* throat. See GAR-
GLE]

Gargoyle, 13th century

(B)

gar·goyle \′gar-,goil\ *n* [ME *gargoyl,*
fr. MF *gargouille;* akin to MF
gargouiller] 1 a : a spout in the
form of a grotesque human or animal
figure projecting from a roof gutter to
throw rainwater clear of a building
b : a grotesquely carved figure 2 : a
person with an ugly face — gar·goyled
\-,goild\ *adj*

gargoyle 1a

(D)

Entries for the word *gargoyle* from leading desk dictionaries: (A) By
permission. From *Webster's New World Dictionary of the American
Language,* college edition, copyright 1964 by the World Publishing
Company, Cleveland, Ohio. (B) By permission. From *The American
College Dictionary,* copyright 1965 by Random House, Inc., New
York. (C) By permission. From *Funk & Wagnalls Standard College
Dictionary,* copyright 1966 by Funk & Wagnalls Company, Inc.,
New York. (D) By permission. From *Webster's Seventh New Col-
legiate Dictionary,* copyright 1965 by G & C Merriam Company.
Publishers of the Merriam-Webster Dictionaries.

2. *Clarity of definition.* Ideally, a good definition should tell you concisely and clearly about an entry in words which you can understand. It should include all senses of the entry word and should distinguish them clearly.

3. *The format.* As we have noted already, dictionaries may present the material in varying ways. Choose the dictionary whose format seems most convenient for you to use. Do you prefer to have the most common meanings of a word listed first in the entry? Does one system of indicating pronunciation seem to be easier to use than another? Is it more convenient to find information when it is all alphabetized together in the body of the text, or do you prefer to have nonlexical information such as place names and biographical names listed separately in the back? Is the print readable without eyestrain? Questions like these will help you decide.

4. *The amount of information which the dictionary contains.* Generally, dictionaries of comparable price give you about the same number of entries. One may claim to have more entries than any other, but this claim may be valid only because miscellaneous information such as names of people and places is not listed separately. Instead, these names are mixed in with the regular word list and counted as entries. All dictionaries do, however, give useful supplementary information. One desk dictionary, newly revised, makes a point of claiming that it is "the only student-oriented desk dictionary" because of the supplementary information which it contains. Before choosing a dictionary on this basis, you should compare several books and decide which contains the most useful information for you.

5. *The attention given to etymologies.* All desk dictionaries give word derivations, but some stress etymology more than others. One dictionary makes a point of tracing a word back to its Indo-European base whenever possible, and the editors pride themselves on the arrangement of the definitions, which follows the etymology and continues to show the semantic development of the word. If you find word histories to be of special interest, this factor should weigh heavily with you.

Exercises

1. For purposes of comparison, look up *tontine, photodynamic,* and *psychodrama* in any two of the dictionaries discussed in this sec-

tion. (If it is not possible to procure any of these, use whatever dictionaries are available.) Which dictionary gives you the clearer definition for each word? Which gives you the most complete definition? Select two words of your own choosing and apply the same questions to them.

2. Look up the following slang terms in several dictionaries to see if they are included as entries (some dictionaries are more liberal in their policy of admitting slang than are others.):

tootsy	topkick	rotgut	paddy wagon	con man
groovy	acid	with it	freak out	cool

Do the same with a slang term of your own choosing. Try to think of reasons why editors don't put all slang terms into their dictionaries.

3. Look up the word *colonel* in both dictionaries. Does either one make any attempt to explain why the pronunciation is so much at variance with the spelling?

4. Look up the word *drag* in both dictionaries. Compare each entry in respect to etymology, order of definition, and completeness of definition. Does each list all the meanings which the other has?

5. Do the same with another common word of your own choosing.

6. Look up these newer words in your dictionaries: *dropout, nose cone, sit-in, teach-in, splashdown, summit* (in the sense of a top-level meeting), *backlash, miniaturize, no-show, drip-dry, glitch, peralun, apalun, destruct, freebie* (slang), *acid* (meaning LSD), *condominium* (meaning a cooperatively-owned apartment house).

7. Which of the two dictionaries has had the most recent revision?

8. Check the entries listed in each book from *dominant* to *dormouse*. Do they include the same words, or do they differ?

9. How many words does each claim to contain?

10. Which book has the most readable, least eyestraining print?

11. Compare the supplementary information, such as tables, charts, and essays, in each dictionary. Which has more information of this sort? Which is the most useful or interesting, in your opinion?

12. Which dictionary would you consider to be the better? Why?

4. Unabridged Dictionaries

As the name suggests, an unabridged dictionary is an un-shortened one. Theoretically, it is a complete record of all the words in use; actually, no dictionary contains *all* the words in the language. One reason is that a dictionary is always working behind the processes of word creation, and countless new words come into use which never make it into the latest lexicon. For another reason, much specialized language—slang, argot, jargon, technical terms— is too limited in use to be included in a general dictionary. Though an unabridged dictionary contains roughly a half million entries, there must be at least another half million words and meanings not included. But at any rate, an unabridged dictionary is the most nearly complete description of words in use available to us.

These books are most useful to professional writers, scholars, technicians, and serious students of language. They provide a great quantity of basic information about a word: its origin, meaning, ancestry, pronunciation, cognates, usage, synonyms, homonyms, grammatical function, spelling, hyphenation, capitalization, and derived forms. They discuss a word in a depth impossible in a desk dictionary. An unabridged dictionary will contain many words and meanings seldom used or no longer in use and, con- versely, many which are so new or specialized that the average reader may never see them in print elsewhere. Between these ex- tremes will fall those words which are more common to our speaking and reading vocabularies. In most homes an unabridged dictionary is a luxury item, since its price is between thirty and fifty dollars. It is an indispensable resource, however, for any school library.

The best-known unabridged dictionaries today are G. & C. Mer- riam Company's *Webster's New International Dictionary*, Second Edition (600,000 entries); its successor, *Webster's Third New Inter- national Dictionary* (450,000 entries); Funk and Wagnalls' *The New Standard Dictionary* (458,000 entries); and *The Random House Dictionary* (260,000 entries). Others on the market include *The New Century Dictionary*, *Webster's New Twentieth Century Dic- tionary*, and *The World Book Dictionary*, which appears to be a simplified "unabridged" for the use of grade school and high school students.

Both the Merriam and Funk and Wagnalls dictionaries have been around for some time. The Merriam books trace their line to Noah Webster's dictionary of 1828 and have had seven major re- visions since that time, the last two in 1934 and 1961. Until the 1897 edition the publishers retained the old title, *An American Dictionary of the English Language* (it was familiarly known as "Webster's

"nabridged"), but after that date they dropped the word *American*
n the title and substituted the word *International*.

The Funk and Wagnalls' *Standard Dictionary of the English
Language* appeared first in 1893 and was edited by Dr. Isaac Kauff-
man Funk. Succeeding editions have appeared periodically with
ew information. Its last revision was in 1959.

The Random House Dictionary (1966) has proved to be a re-
pected and highly successful competitor to the other two un-
bridged dictionaries. It is probably the only unabridged to appear
n households in large numbers, since it was promoted commercially
hrough a Book-of-the-Month Club tieup and could be obtained
or only five dollars if one joined the club. Among its features are
extensive encyclopedic materials and a special supplement which
gives the key vocabularies of French, Spanish, German, and Italian.
This supplement is arranged in each case for two-way reference,
hat is, from the foreign language into English and vice versa.

Anyone going on to college, entering a job field which requires
working with words, or just having a strong interest in the language,
vill need to become familiar with the unabridged dictionary. It is
nore cumbersome than a desk dictionary, but it contains a great
deal more information, gathered and synthesized by experts and
unavailable anywhere else in one volume.

For further reading on this subject, see the pertinent introduc-
ory' articles in the front of any of the desk dictionaries discussed
n this chapter. They are the most current and concise handling of
he subject available anywhere and are very readable. Also see
Chapter 29 of *American English in Its Cultural Setting* by Donald
J. Lloyd and Harry R. Warfel (New York: Alfred A. Knopf, Inc.,
1957) and *Words: How to Know Them* by M. M. Mathews (New
York: Holt, Rinehart & Winston, Inc., 1956).

5. Special Dictionaries

In addition to the general dictionaries which we have been discussing in this chapter, there are many special dictionaries as well.
What makes a dictionary "special"? Instead of treating all kinds
of words, it concentrates exclusively on a particular part of language or knowledge. If you browse through a large metropolitan
library, you may see on the reference shelves literally dozens of
different special dictionaries, treating such diverse topics as archi-

tecture, engineering, ballet, botany, cooking, gardening, foreign languages, photography, gems, jazz, slang, similes, and clichés. The word *dictionary* applies loosely to some of these; *encyclopedia* might describe their function more nearly, since they report at some length on each entry. For example, in the *Dictionary of World Literature* a discussion of French literature covers fifteen and one-half pages. Still, they are all dictionaries in the sense that they arrange their entries alphabetically and emphasize at least one of a dictionary's functions, usually definition. A few kinds of these special dictionaries are discussed in the sections that follow.

6. Dictionaries of Slang

Any use of language by a group of people on any level is worthy of study. Slang, which many people consider to be on the border of respectable language, has been the subject of several important dictionaries because it is a part of our language which needs to be recorded.

An important dictionary of this kind is *A Dictionary of Slang and Unconventional English,* edited by an Englishman, Eric Partridge. It was first printed in 1937 and revised in 1950. Volume I is made up of 1,362 pages and contains 100,000 slang terms. Volume II, a supplement, contains many of the newer slang terms that have entered the language during the past thirty years. Designed to be a companion to the *OED*, it encompasses all terms in the language other than standard and dialectical uses. About 50 percent of the entries are slang and argot, while 35 percent are colloquialisms. Argot is the special language of a clique or other closely knit group —the language of the underworld, for example. Colloquialisms are informal words and phrases, found more frequently in conversation than in writing. Unlike many slang expressions, they have acquired permanence in the language and are widely used.

Another slang lexicon is *The American Thesaurus of Slang* by Lester V. Berrey and Melvin Van den Bark, first published in 1942 and revised in 1952. As one thumbs through this very complete categorization of slang terms, certain conclusions are inescapable:

1. The total effect of a slang dictionary is depressing. Most of our slang terms name unpleasant things or are terms of personal disparagement. Human nature takes a beating here.

2. The English language has a great capacity for invention; there are 940 pages of slang words and expressions.

3. Most slang is short-lived, and, like cant and jargon, is often the special language of a group. Teenagers, athletes, musicians, car enthusiasts, businessmen, truckdrivers, cooks, moviemakers—each group is likely to have its own slang vocabulary. Even within one group the expressions seldom remain constant. Any GI of World War II can tell you what *chow* means, but only a soldier who has been in Vietnam will know what is meant by *arc light* (a B-52 strike), *the world* (home), *higher-higher* (commanding superior), *Charlie* or *the little people* (the enemy), *newbie* (a just-arrived soldier), *short-timer* (one with 120 days or less to serve in Vietnam), and *fast-movers* (helicopter pilots' designation for jet planes). If a slang dictionary were to be really up-to-date, it would require monthly revision, since slang, more than any other kind of word, is transitory. True, a few slang words like *mob, okay,* and *guts* find a permanent niche in the language, but the typical slang word is more like Shakespeare's "poor player" who "struts and frets his hour upon the stage and then is heard no more."

4. Slang gives us an opportunity to play with words and ideas. Notice these food orders turned into slang: "Adam and Eve on a raft—wreck 'em (make two scrambled eggs on toast); "make it cackle" (add eggs to an order); "hitch old Dobbin to a bun" (make a hamburger sandwich); "clean up the kitchen" or "the gentleman says he will take a chance" (serve hash); and "put out the lights and cry" (add onion).

The most recent slang dictionary is *The Dictionary of American Slang*, edited by Harold Wentworth and Stuart Berg Flexner and published in 1960. It is also a scholarly work, but is nevertheless so "eyebrow raising" in its frank inclusion of all common slang terms that some public librarians keep the book off the reference shelf, and check it out only from the desk upon demand. Most high school libraries do not carry it at all, for the same reason.

A quick journey through its pages reveals that the word having the most slang synonyms is *drunk* (327 synonyms are listed), that many towns have slang nicknames (Beantown, Cincy, Chi, Big Windy, Derbyville, Stirville), and that many slang terms begin with the preposition *on:*

on the ball, on the beam, on the blink, on the bottle, on the bum, on the button, on the carpet, on the cuff, on the dot, on the double, on the fire, on the fritz, on the go, on the house, on the lam, on the level, on the mat, on the nose, on the pan, on the rocks, on the ropes, on the shelf, on the skids, on the spot, on the stick, on the town, on the up and up, on the wagon . . .

The volume also introduces us to cockney rhyming slang, a device of subterfuge which substitutes a rhymed expression for the word that is really intended. Thus, *feet* becomes *plates of meat*, *room* becomes *shovel and broom,* and *wife* becomes *trouble and strife.*

7.   Dictionaries of American English

There are two outstanding dictionaries of American English. The first, *A Dictionary of American English on Historical Principles* (1944), is a four-volume set which explores the origins of American words and expressions just as the *OED* does for the English language as a whole. It defines and dates the early occurrences in American English of such words as *bushwhacker, canyon, canvasback, carbine, carpetbagger, caucus,* and *celery,* to name a few at random. This work of scholarship is limited to words which appeared first in American English. It does not deal with new words which came into English after the end of the nineteenth century.

The other outstanding book of this type is *A Dictionary of Americanisms on Historical Principles* (1951) in two volumes, edited by Mitford M. Mathews. It follows the path created by the *DAE,* but modifies some of the earlier book's findings in the light of more recent scholarship. The very first entry, the letter *A,* tells us that the use of this letter to denote a grade for superior work was an American innovation, first made in 1877 at Augustana College in Illinois. Other firsts sampled from Volume One include the term *road agent* for *highwayman, clerk* (to designate one who waits on customers in a store), *dorg* for *dog, dorm* for *dormitory, doughboy* as a term for *soldier, graft* (to describe a shady means of getting money), and *graduate* as a verb meaning "to complete an elementary or high school course." Multiply these examples by the thousands and you have a rough idea of how many words and meanings are native only to American English.

8. Other Kinds of Special Dictionaries

Here in brief are a number of other dictionaries which deal with language in a special way.

1. *The English Dialect Dictionary*, edited by Joseph Wright and published in six volumes, is an important work of scholarship. It covers dialect in use during the eighteenth and nineteenth centuries in the British Isles.

We do not yet have a comparable work for American English, but with the backing of the American Dialect Society and a half-million-dollar grant from the government, work began on one in 1967. Frederic G. Cassidy of the Universiy of Wisconsin heads "Project DARE" (*Dictionary of American Regional English*) and hopes that the dictionary will be in print by 1976. Graduate English students from the university armed with tape recorders and lengthy questionnaires have gone to over 1000 communities in all fifty states to interview people about their language. Information has also been gathered from the written language of particular regions. To the surprise of no one, the project is showing that regional variations still exist, especially in rural areas. In parts of Alabama the word *bushwhacking* means "to haul a boat along a stream by pulling on low branches," in parts of the Southwest a *nightingale* is a burro, and in parts of Arkansas a *waiter* is a best man at a wedding.

2. There are literally hundreds of English–foreign language dictionaries which provide foreign meanings for English words and English meanings for foreign words. They vary in scope and scholarship. Some are designed only to meet the needs of the casual traveler in a foreign land and supply him with handy words and phrases like "Where can I get an American sandwich?" Others, written for the serious student of language, are comprehensive. Currently, dictionaries are in print which translate English into Afrikaans, Assamese, Chinook, Coptic, Czech, Greek (both old and new), Gaelic, Icelandic, Interlingua (an artificial "universal language"), Sanskrit, Swahili, Tagalog, Urdu, Vietnamese, Zulu, and forty-four other languages.

3. One way to handle problems that come up regarding "proper grammar" is to consult a dictionary of English usage. These books discuss questions like the following: Can a sentence be started with *and* or *but*? When do you use *bad* and when do you use *badly*?

Can *imply* and *infer* be used interchangeably? Is it all right to say *try and* instead of *try to*?

One book, Margaret M. Bryant's *Current American Usage* (1962), represents a liberal and impersonal approach to such matters. Using evidence gathered from actual published writing, and bringing to bear reports from language scholars, the book describes and summarizes the current status of disputed usages. The studies in the book disclose, for instance, that reputable writers do begin sentences with *and* or *but*, concluding that this "construction is used in the best writing." Here usage rests on actual and documented custom, rather than on what Miss Bryant thinks it should be.

The authoritarian approach to usage—discussions and judgments on usage problems by a knowledgeable author—is found in these well-known volumes: *Concise Usage, A Modern Guide to Usage and Abusage*, by Eric Partridge; *A Dictionary of American Usage*, by Margaret Nicholson; *Hook's Guide to Good Writing*, by J. N. Hook; *A Dictionary of Contemporary American Usage*, by Bergen and Cornelia Evans; *A Dictionary of Modern American Usage*, by H. W. Horwill; *Modern American Usage*, by Wilson Follett (the most recent book); and the best-known of them all, *A Dictionary of Modern English Usage*, by the Englishman, H. W. Fowler, recently revised by Ernest Gowers, but first published in 1926.

This last book, in particular, is a delight to read because it bears the mark of Fowler's positive personality and his firm convictions about how the language should be used. The headings are unscientific but intriguing. Under the heading "Superstitions," he tells us that we should throw out the notions that sentences cannot be started with *but*, that sentences cannot be ended with prepositions, and that infinitives cannot be split. His little essay on the whole question of the split infinitive shows that he can treat a potentially dry subject with humor. Here is a beginning excerpt:

> The English-speaking world may be divided into (1) those who neither know nor care what a split infinitive is; (2) those who do not know, but care very much; (3) those who know and condemn; (4) those who know and approve; and (5) those who know and distinguish.
>
> 1. Those who neither know nor care are the vast majority, and are a happy folk, to be envied by most of the minority classes. . . .
>
> 2. To the second class, those who do not know but do care, who would as soon be caught putting their knives in their mouths as split-

ting an infinitive but have hazy notions of what constitutes that de‑
plorable breach of etiquette, this article is chiefly addressed.[1]

Fowler's work is more than a reference book; it is good reading
as well.

4. Another kind of special dictionary is the dictionary of pro‑
nunciation. The best known are *The Pronunciation of English*, by
Daniel Jones; *A Pronouncing Dictionary of American English*, by
John S. Kenyon and Thomas A. Knott; and *The NBC Handbook of
Pronunciation*, by Thomas L. Crowell, Jr.

5. There are many books which tell stories of curious word
origins, but very few etymological dictionaries: *An Etymological
Dictionary of the English Language*, by W. W. Skeat (this is avail‑
able also in a concise edition); *Origins: A Short Etymological Dictionary of Modern English*, by Eric Partridge; and *A Dictionary of
Word Origins*, by Joseph T. Shipley.

6. Of all the dictionaries of synonyms, and there have been
many over a long period of time, the most famous was *Roget's
Thesaurus of English Words and Phrases*, first published in 1852.
Now, apparently, the word *Roget*, like *Webster*, may be attached to
any publisher's thesaurus. Of the twenty-six word-finder books on
the market today, ten have the name *Roget* in their titles. Another
name which helps sell a thesaurus is *Soule*. *Soule's Dictionary of
Synonyms*, a respected competitor of Roget, first appeared in 1871.
Books of synonyms containing Soule's name also appear on the
modern market. Comprehensive and modern approaches to syn‑
onymy are contained in *Webster's Dictionary of Synonyms* (Mer‑
riam, 1942) and in the *Modern Guide to Synonyms* (Funk and
Wagnalls, 1968). The latter book is the work of the well-known
semanticist, S. I. Hayakawa, and it reflects his belief that many of
the world's troubles would be avoided if people could choose words
that communicated precise shades of meaning.

7. A miscellaneous collection of other special dictionaries would
include the *Rhyming Dictionary of the English Language*, the
Oxford Dictionary of Quotations, *Bartlett's Familiar Quotations*,
the *Dictionary of American Proverbs*, the *Dictionary of Obsolete
English*, the *Dictionary of Clichés*, *Webster's Geographical Dictionary*, *Webster's Biographical Dictionary*, and even a *Dictionary of
Occupational Titles*.

---

[1] Reprinted by permission of the Clarendon Press, Oxford.

This last dictionary provides fun for word-watchers because of the off-beat job titles which are listed. Out of the 36,000 in the whole two-volume set are titles like "squeak-rattle and leak man" (an auto mechanic for test runs), "keep-off girl" (a special insurance clerk), "leg inspector" (worker in a stocking factory), "cracker stacker," and "bologna lacer."

Exercises

1. Visit your school or public library and examine the special dictionaries available for your use.

2. Pick out any common word and compare the entries for it in both a desk and unabridged dictionary.

3. Compare the number of entries between the words *idea* and *identity* in both a desk and an unabridged dictionary.

4. Compare the usage entry for *ain't* in both a desk dictionary and an unabridged dictionary.

5. Compare the entries for *try and*, *any more*, and the use of *like* as a preposition in Bryant's *Current American Usage* and any other usage book mentioned in this chapter.

6. Examine carefully *Roget's Thesaurus* or any other synonym finder and be prepared to explain how it is used. (For example, how does one find a synonym for *black* in *Roget*?)

8

Making a Modern Dictionary

1. Citations and Definitions

It took twenty-seven years and $3,500,000 to produce; a hundred editors and scores of consultants gave their time to it. It weighs thirteen and one-half pounds, is four and one-half inches thick, and you can take it home for under $50. It is the most accurate and comprehensive record of current English in the world today. The book—G. & C. Merriam Company's *Third New International Dictionary*—is the eighth in a series of dictionaries which began with Noah Webster's big one of 1828. Because it represents the latest thought and technique in scientific lexicography, we are going to take a close look at W3, as it will be called for the sake of convenience, to see how a modern dictionary is made. Perhaps we can also arrive at a clear understanding of what a dictionary is, and is not, designed to do.

One of the most remarkable facts about this book is that it is completely new. Every single definition for all 450,000 entries was written from scratch—a task seldom attempted in lexicography. W3 has fewer pages than its predecessor, *Webster's Second International Dictionary* (2,720 pages to 3,194 pages), but over 100,000 new words have been added. It made room for them by omitting obsolete and archaic words coined before 1755, the date of Johnson's dictionary. The new words include a tremendous number spawned by science since 1934 (the date of the last edition, W2) as well as new words and meanings from all areas of modern life. Here is just a small sampling of new words in W3.

Scientific Terms	Political and Social Terms	Slang
antiproton	megalopolis	headshrinker
bubble chamber	Sovietologist	payola
DNA	brainwashing	wolf whistle
earth science	big lie	shindig
thermal barrier	brinksmanship	gabby
antimatter	escalation	wacky
astronaut	explosion (population)	nudnik
astronavigation	multilateralism	fuddy-duddy
blast-off	sit-in	hep
sputnik	beatnik	square
pad	doublethink	hepster
fallout	supermarket	in the groove
spectogram	double-talk	palooka
hydrocortisone	summitry	pad

It has been claimed that more words have entered the language during the past fifty years than during any other period, except perhaps the periods just before Chaucer and Shakespeare. Incidentally, the longest word in the dictionary is no longer *antidisestablishmentarianism.* The new jawbreaker is *pneumonoultramicroscopicsilicovolcanoconiosis,* and if you want to know what it means you will have to look it up in W3. The last word in the dictionary is *zyzzeton,* a large South American leafhopper.

The dictionary editors found the words and meanings to put into their book by literally looking for them. Editors, research assistants, and hundreds of unpaid word-watchers throughout the country read countless numbers of newspapers, magazines, books, and other kinds of printed materials. They hunted for new words and new meanings present in old words. Every time they found one, they recorded it on a citation slip. Suppose an editor found an occurrence of the word *piggyback* in a sentence from a railroad pamphlet. He would fill out a citation slip that might have looked like this:

---

piggyback   Date: May 1, 1959

Source: pamphlet, *Union Pacific Notes*

"The trailer rode piggyback from coast to coast."

Thus each citation slip contained a sampling of a word as it was used in print. One or two slips per word was not enough evidence for a word's inclusion in the dictionary. A substantial number had to be accumulated; the number of slips for some words ran into the hundreds, largely because many words have more than one meaning or sense. The seemingly simple word *set*, for instance, fills three columns in W3.

As these citations were collected, they were classified and filed away to become raw material for the writing of word definitions. Over four and one-half million were collected in this manner by the staff between 1934 and 1959. Others were taken over from the files of W2 and other established reference sources. Eventually the total for all words reached ten million, the greatest single collection of word samplings in the history of the world!

These ten million became the basis for the 450,000 word entries. How? The staff studied the slips for each separate meaning of a word and formulated a definition for each, deciding what each meaning was by the way the word was used in the citations. Each definition was thus based upon the way the word was actually being used in the language, not upon the way the editors thought it ought to be used. They did not discriminate good words, fancy words, poor words, slang words, and so on. A word got into the dictionary if there was evidence that it was being spoken or written by an adequate number of people. The aim was a comprehensive record of current English.

After the definitions were written, much had still to be done. Each entry required decisions as to the arrangement of meanings, the word's pronunciation, grammatical function, capitalization, history, and spelling. Then came months of tedious cross-checking, cross-referencing, proofing, correcting, and revising before the book was ready for the presses. Merriam Company estimates that it would have taken one editor, working alone, over 757 years to accomplish all the editorial work.

W3 followed accepted dictionary practice in providing illustrative quotations to back up some of the definitions and to show how the words are used in sentences. From the file of citations they selected 200,000 sentences, using them where they were most needed to reinforce a meaning. The quotations came from 14,000 individuals and several hundred publications. Here is an example of one which was used to document one of the fifteen recorded senses for the word *puff*:

> to praise extravagantly: OVERRATE, EXTOLL
> (hit too many homers and people start puffing you up—Willie Mays)

Notice that a word can be defined, as this one is, in three different ways—by a defining phrase, by a synonym, and by its use in context.

You can run into some interesting people in W3. We have already met Willie Mays; others who appear by way of example sentences for word meaning include Burl Ives, President Eisenhower, President Kennedy, Sir Winston Churchill, Willa Cather, Jack Kerouac, Art Linkletter, and Pearl Buck. Jimmy Durante, the comedian who murders the king's English, is also cited, but so are Shakespeare, Shaw, Milton, and the Bible. This is not to say that only famous people are cited. Most of the illustrations come from writers and publications whose business is working with the written word.

Quotations from a variety of publications are included. *The New York Times* is most often used (over 700 times), and many other newspapers are quoted also. So are all these publications and scores of others: *Time, Life, The Congressional Record, Downbeat, The Reader's Digest*, the *Sears Roebuck Catalog* (and numerous college catalogs), *The New Yorker, Scholastic Coach, Harpers, Infantry Journal, Annual Report of J. C. Penney Company*, and the old barbershop favorite, *The Police Gazette*. Different as they are in content, they all have one thing in common. They furnished examples of the language in use, of Americans communicating with other Americans in the language of their time. Of course, the editors could have restricted their selection, taking only citations from literature of a certain kind or level, or perhaps from a select list of "the hundred best writers," but this would not have done the job they wanted to do. They felt that it was their responsibility to record the living language, not just the best language.

2. Pronunciation

The editors had similar convictions about recording pronunciation. They knew that it would be unrealistic to insist that there was only one, standard way to pronounce a word (what do *you* say, "creek" or "crick"?). Recognizing that there is now a wide variety of regional pronunciations in this country, they listed all the major ones for each word. They included those which are in actual use by a sufficient number of cultivated speakers in any region, whether it be the North, New England, the Midland, the South, the West, the Southwest, or the Northwest. This policy suggests that a pronunciation is correct if it is an accepted one for a particular area.

Have you ever noticed that you can and do pronounce the same words differently? Standing on a platform, making a speech, you might say "Feb'ru·ary," making sure that the *r* in the middle is enunciated. But in casual conversation with your friends, you might say it "Feb'u·ary," as many people do. *W3* took pains to find out how people pronounce words informally, "off the platform." They went directly to the speakers of the language, surveying their pronunciation by monitoring radio and television speech, taking language samples on tape, and listening to people speak in a variety of speech situations. They used dialect studies and other results of modern linguistic scholarship as well. The editors found that these methods gave them accurate information about how words are pronounced in everyday speech. Their authority for assigning pronunciations to words is thus based upon close observation of the way that cultivated people speak in informal situations.

3. Labels

Giving accurate information about the current status of a word is just about the most chancy business a dictionary can undertake. Words are like people—they can change their neighborhoods and frequently do; yesterday's slang may be tomorrow's usage, and a word which is current today may be obsolete fifty years hence. Even nonstandard usage may have its ups and downs. *Ain't*, for example, was a perfectly acceptable word in the eighteenth century. It appears frequently in the writing of Jonathan Swift, author of *Gulliver's Travels*. Then its reputation began to decline, and now any schoolboy can tell us that *ain't* is bad grammar. But perhaps its use is going to become more respectable in the future: *W3* found that *ain't* is being used by a significant number of reputable speakers in the expression "ain't I," so the dictionary statement about the word's use had to be qualified to that degree.

Labels are useful when you want to know in what context a word's use is appropriate. The trouble is that such labels are frequently misunderstood because many people do not take the time to read the explanations for them in the dictionary introduction. For example, many people misunderstand the label "colloquial" when it is attached to a word. "Colloquial" means that the word is most often used informally or in conversation; it does not mean that a word is inferior and hence to be avoided, or that it is a dialectal word used only in a certain part of the country.

The editors of W3 omitted the label "colloquial" entirely because, as they state, "it is too hard to tell whether a word out of context is colloquial or not." At any rate, the reader must realize that a standard (unlabeled) word may be as formal as *celebration* or as informal as *shindig*.

Keeping their labels to a minimum, W3's editors settled upon these as being sufficient for all words and senses needing special comment about their usage:

Archaic	This label refers to words and to senses relatively common in an earlier time, but infrequently used today. Archaic terms survive in old literature (the Bible, Shakespeare) and are used occasionally by modern writers who wish to achieve special effects.
	Examples: *belike, prithee, doth, thou, eftsoons, eke, ekename, weigh* (archaic when it means "to heave or hoist" anything other than an anchor).
Obsolete	This label refers to an old word or meaning no longer in use.
	Examples: *abhorrency, absume, tent* (in the sense of "to probe"), *swoopstake* (an obsolete form of *sweepstake*), *danger* (in the sense of "the range of a weapon"), and *quaint* in the sense of "cunning, scheming, crafty").

Slang	Slang, according to W3, is hard to pin down, but is characterized by extreme informality, forced figures of speech, shortened forms of words, quick popularity, and often quick oblivion. These words —all out of their normal, standard context—currently carry a slang meaning of approval: *cool, tough, neat, something else, hot*. Sometimes slang becomes standard if it survives; *mob, banter, bully,* and *sham* were all slang in the eighteenth century.
Substandard	This label refers to a word which is in use, but is not used by cultivated speakers of the language.
	Examples: *hisself, brung, drownded*. Other dictionaries use labels such as *illiterate* or *vulgar* for words like these. (Question: Does *substandard* refrain from making a value judgment as these terms do?)
Nonstandard	This term refers to a word which is not recognized in standard usage, but which appears, nevertheless, in the language of some speakers of cultivated English.
	Example: *irregardless*.
Dialect (and other regional labels)	These labels indicate specific regional patterns (*West*), complex regional patterns that cannot be pinned down to a special locale (*dial*), a British dialect (*dial Brit*), and standard patterns peculiar to other English-speaking countries (*chiefly Scot*).
	Examples: *cayuse* (*West*), *jaybird* (*chiefly Midland*), *bodacious* (*South and South Midland*), *britches* (*dial*), *larrup* (*dial*), *top-hole* (*chiefly Brit*), *petrol* (*Brit*).

Any word which does not have any of these status labels is considered to be in standard usage. It is important to remember, too, that a label often applies to only one meaning of a particular word, and that the other meanings may be standard.

4. Capitalization

W3 has a method of indicating capitalized words which is different from that used in other dictionaries. Instead of printing the entry word in caps if it is commonly capitalized, W3 prints all words lower case and indicates capitalization by one of four labels. The label *cap* means that a word is almost always capitalized initially. The label *usu cap* indicates that a word is capitalized more often than not; the label *often cap* means that a word is acceptable one way or the other; the label *sometimes cap* means that a word is usually not capitalized, but may be found capitalized occasionally.

These designations enable the editors to record capitalization usage honestly. The reader may complain that he would prefer a straight "yes or no" statement, but the truth is that a "yes or no" statement about a word's capitalization cannot always be made. This area of usage, like others, does not remain static. It is interesting to compare current textbook rules on capitalization with W3's designations for certain words.

These, in brief, are some of the features of this unabridged dictionary. In principle, it was made as all good modern dictionaries are made: through a painstaking, meticulous process of recording, analyzing, defining, and labeling words.

And what of the future? In an age of automation and computer technology, will advanced methods of information storage and retrieval make the unabridged dictionary obsolete? Will the definition-seeker of the future sit at a desk in the public library, press the right buttons, and be fed the latest word information from memory banks which can be kept constantly current?

Definitely not, according to Dr. Philip Gove, editor of W3. Dr. Gove feels that technology, no matter how advanced, will never replace the familiar unabridged dictionary. It is true, however, that since the publication of W3, the dictionary-making process has been speeded up by technology. More recent dictionaries than W3 have, to some degree, used the computer in the typesetting and editing tasks.

The computer has also proved capable of doing word analyses— the kind of research that can be of great help to a lexicographer. It has been used, for example, to count how many times each word appears in a large body of material. The results, incidentally, showed that out of a million words found in a representative body of text there were only 50,406 different words. The computer revealed that the most frequently used words were *the* (69,971 times), *of* (36,411 times), *and* (28,852 times), *to* (26,149 times), *a* (23,237 times), *in* (21,341 times), *that* (10,595 times), *is* (10,099 times), *was* (9,816 times), and *he* (9,543 times).

Computers have also produced concordances, which not only list the occurrence of each different word in a body of print, but also record the context (the sentence or line in which the word appears). Computers may also be programmed to search out and list all occurrences of any particular word which a lexicographer might be interested in to make them quickly available for studies of their use and meaning. Computers can also store word information in their memory banks of wire or tape, making obsolete the lexicographer's innumerable cards and files for citations. With word information stored in a computer's memory banks, an editor can have any item flashed on a video screen for checking, and he can correct it or change it, if need be, right on the screen.

5. The *W3* Controversy

One would think that a dictionary like this would have been greeted with unanimous praise when published in 1961. After all, it was a major achievement in scholarship, reflecting principles in dictionary making which lexicographers had been subscribing to for years. The reaction was mixed, however. Several magazine reviewers responded in print to W3 as if it were the Bible newly rewritten to take an approving view of sin! Many newspaper reviewers then echoed their cry, and called the book variously "a calamity," "an exponent of anarchy in language," and "a disaster."

What was all the excitement about? Basically, these reviewers did not like W3 because it is not an authoritarian dictionary. They did not think that a dictionary should tell them what the language is; they wanted it to tell them what it should be. The dictionary, the critics insisted, has a responsibility to set forth and try to maintain high standards of usage for the language. It should use its authority and prestige to resist changes which tend to alter these standards. W3 did not do this, they claimed.

And, of course, they were right. W3 is not an authoritarian dictionary—most dictionaries have not been for some time. Its announced intention was to collect and present information about the language, rather than to mold it. As its editor, Dr. Philip Gove, stated: "The responsibility of a dictionary is to record the language, not set its style." He, along with most modern language scholars and lexicographers, believed that a dictionary must *describe* the language, not *prescribe* what it should be.

About this basic difference in philosophy, arguments were carried on; attacks and counterattacks were made in the editorial and literary review pages of magazines and newspapers across the country. It is impossible to report all the comments made, but these were the major complaints about W3:

1. It contained vulgar and illiterate words and expressions, including, in the words of *Life* magazine, "that most monstrous of all non-words—*irregardless.*"

2. It did not tell what the critics thought to be the truth about some word usages. For example, alarums and excursions were set off in newspapers by part of W3's comment about the word *ain't:* "used orally in most parts of the U.S. by many cultivated speakers of the language."

3. It did not try to discriminate between good and bad English.

"*Sorry. Dr. Gove ain't in.*"

Drawing by Alan Dunn; © 1962 by The New Yorker Magazine, Inc.

It merely "counted noses," and it implied by its permissive attitude that whatever is, is right.

4. It did not use strong enough labels for words that the critics considered to be poor usage. Traditional labels such as "vulgar," "illiterate," and "erroneous" were replaced in *W3* by "nonstandard" and "substandard."

5. The omission of the "colloquial" label was a hardship on the reader. He wants to be told when a word is used formally or informally.

6. The critics believed that illustrative citations should be taken only from the works of the best writers in the history of the language, past and present. Many of *W3*'s citations, they claimed, were taken from mediocre sources. Some of the people whose words were used to illustrate definitions were not good writers or speakers —Ethel Merman, Jimmy Durante, Willie Mays, and Art Linkletter, for example.

7. *W3* did not tell you the names of the apostles or who the Virgin Mary was. (*W3* omitted the biographical section which appeared in its predecessor, on the grounds that a dictionary's true function is to deal with words, not people.)

However, not all reviewers were critical. Those who were familiar with developments in the science of language during the past hundred years praised and defended *W3*. They agreed with the editor that a dictionary must tell the truth about the way language behaves, regardless of whose notions are upset. Today's language, they said, is not the language of 1934, and to treat it as if it were would not be honest. One way of explaining the point of view of the language scholar and of *W3* is to amplify five short statements about language endorsed by the National Council of Teachers of English:

1. *Language changes constantly*. Shakespeare would have had difficulty understanding the language of Chaucer in the late 1300's. We have trouble understanding the language of Shakespeare. Yet the language of Chaucer, Shakespeare, and of our own time is all one. It has been in a continuous process of change and development. In a hundred years it may be different from what it is today. A lexicographer cannot keep this change from happening. He cannot preserve or fix the language at the stage of development which he or his age prefers. All he can do is to describe accurately the language of his own time, a tremendous job in itself.

2. *Change is normal.* Each language changes according to its own rules in complex but recognizable ways. New words, new ways of using them, new pronunciations, new grammatical practices will all be a part of the change. This constant change is the reason that new dictionaries are needed periodically.

3. *Spoken language is the language.* Written language came long after speech. Spoken language changes first, and it changes more rapidly than written language. Lexicographers consider colloquial, or spoken, language to be standard and worthy of study. It represents the language in its primary state. Correct pronunciation is determined by popular spoken usage, not by the way a word is spelled.

4. *Correctness rests upon usage.* What is correct is determined by the usage of the cultivated speakers and writers of the language at any given time. It is difficult to tell whether a word is correct or not if it is not considered in its context. A dictionary does not hold to an eternal and "revealed from on high" law of correctness. It records current usage and labels it as well as it can, so that the user can make his own choice. One way that a dictionary can illustrate current usage is to draw upon a variety of speakers and writers for illustrations—even Ethel Merman and Jimmy Durante, if their contextual statements correspond to popular usage.

5. *All usage is relative.* Usage is relative to speaker, time, situation, and place; therefore, one cannot say that the most formal English is always the best English for all occasions. A college professor does not speak like the popular image of a college professor all the time; he may adapt his language to specific situations. Colloquial English is not inferior because it is less formal—it is just another kind of English. Slang has its place and time also. Dialects are standard and acceptable for their geographical areas.

Who are right—the editors of W3 and their academic supporters or the writer-critics who represent the journalistic and literary fraternity? The critics have a point when they say, "This may be a fine dictionary in some respects, but it is too scientific; it doesn't give us all the guidance needed. We want information—authoritative information—about the standings of words. It's a fact of life that some words are in better usage than others, and the reader has a right to know which they are."

On the other hand, W3 is unquestionably an outstanding dictionary when judged by how well it succeeded in doing what it set out to do. It is clear that linguistic scholarship backs up *W3's* descriptive approach to the language. Even rival dictionary editors would agree that a dictionary can only record the language, not regulate it. And many scholars agree with the editors that the whole matter of determining the social status of words is too complex and variable for simplistic decisions. As one distinguished authority, Charlton Laird, puts it: "Good usage requires wide knowledge and tasteful discrimination; it cannot be learned easily . . . . language levels are vague and shifty, and trying to provide labels for them causes gray hair and ulcers in editorial offices."

It is interesting to note, nevertheless, that since the outcry in the press against *W3*, succeeding dictionaries—particularly the *American Heritage Dictionary*—have accepted the role of usage authority. The business of a dictionary publisher is, after all, to sell dictionaries, so the public gets what it wants.

Exercises

Questions 1 through 13 deal with the entries for *board* found at the end of Chapter 6 from *Webster's Third New International Dictionary*.

1. What is the basic difference between the entries for ¹*board* and ²*board?*
2. What information about the word is given between reversed virgules (\   \ )?
3. What information about the word is given between brackets ([ ])?
4. What does the division by numbers within the entry indicate?
5. How many meanings of the word are given in both entries?
6. How is the mark ~ used?
7. Which is an obsolete sense of the word? Archaic? Slang?
8. Find an example of a verbal illustration for one of the senses.
9. Find an example of a name cited for authorship of an illustration.
10. Which meaning is given first in an entry—the earliest or the most common?
11. What kinds of meanings are given at the end of the entry?

12. What did *board* mean in Gothic, Old Norse, and Old High German?

13. Can you illustrate from an examination of the entries that definitions often begin with the same part of speech as the word being defined?

Questions 14 through 20 apply to the three columns of new words found on page 152 of this chapter.

14. Look over the list of words and comment briefly on the context in which you might meet them—a branch of knowledge, a political or social event, and so on.

15. The word *hipster* in W3 is not defined under its own separate entry but is cross-referenced to *hepster* as a mere variant. If the W3 were revised today, do you think that would still be the case? What does your answer imply about the nature of slang?

16. What is the basic connection between the two meanings of the word *pad?*

17. How do you explain the similar endings of *sputnik, beatnik,* and *nudnik?* Have you seen any other words with the *-nik* ending?

18. How many words are composed of separate words put together—either as open compounds, solid compounds, or hyphenated compounds? Is this a popular method of word formation, or is it rare? Using the dictionary or your memory, try to list ten compounds.

19. Which words have been created through the addition of prefixes and suffixes?

20. Consulting your dictionary if necessary, determine which of the words listed are new words that have never appeared in a dictionary before, and which are old words with new meanings.

21. Some critics complained of W3 that it did not label some words "slang" which should have been so labeled. Defenders of W3 replied that slang is difficult to label, that all dictionaries disagree at times on what is slang and what is not. Check three different desk dictionaries to see how they label the following words. If a word is unlabeled, it is considered to be formal standard usage. A "colloquial" label means that the word is informal standard usage.

| pinhead | bonehead | slush fund | enthuse | scads |
| cop | corny | pushover | frisk | vamoose |

Do all three dictionaries agree on the labeling of each word? If there is disagreement, how would you explain it?

The following questions and activities require a visit to a library containing several kinds of unabridged dictionaries. Perhaps individual students will volunteer to report on them.

22. List all unabridged dictionaries available in your library.

23. Check the supplementary information available in W2, W3, the *New Standard*, and the *Random House* dictionaries. Does any one of them contain supplementary tables or materials not available in the others? List them.

24. How does the *New Standard* keep up with new words, since it does not have frequent, large-scale revisions?

25. Do W2 and W3 have the same usage labels for these words: *fox* ("to outwit"), *turn the trick*, *ten-strike* (figurative sense), *enthuse?* If the labeling has changed, how do you account for it?

26. Look up the entry for *ain't* in W3. Copy the part which discusses the use of *ain't*. Do the same for *ain't* in W2. Report to the class on any different statements of usage.

27. Compare the definitions for *door* in W3 and W2. Which definition is easier for you to follow? Which definition gives you more information?

28. Look up *irregardless* in W3. In view of your findings, give your reaction to this criticism of W3 from the *American Bar Journal:* "Perhaps the most flagrant example of lexicographic irresponsibility is the undiscriminating listing of 'that most monstrous of all nonwords, *irregardless.*'" (The journal is quoting from an article in *Life.*)

29. Compare the order of definition for *board* in W3 and Funk and Wagnalls' *New Standard Dictionary* (unabridged). Report to the class on the difference.

30. The following statements all relate in some way to the W3 controversy. Assume that you are the editor of W3 and explain why you would agree or disagree with each statement.

    a. "Language, be it remember'd, is not an abstract construction of the learn'd, or of dictionary-makers, but is something arising out of the work, needs, ties, joys, affections, tastes, of long generations of humanity, and has its bases broad and low, close to the ground." —Walt Whitman (1819–1892).

b. "A dictionary is a malevolent literary device for cramping the growth of a language and making it hard and inelastic." —Ambrose Bierce (1842–1914).

c. "His [the lexicographer's] function is to record rather what the language is than what it ought to be." —"Preface," *Webster's International Dictionary of the English Language*, 1897 edition.

d. "Regrettably, it must be accepted that such endorsement as that of Chief Justice Warren is enough to admit the misused word [*hopefully*] to Webster's. Thus does the high court change the language, as it changes the law." —From a newspaper, *The Oregonian*, in an editorial condemning the use of the word *hopefully* (instead of the expression "it is hoped that") in an important written decision by Chief Justice Warren.

e. "Similarly, those who look up words in a dictionary, like those who consult a doctor, are seeking authority; they want the doctor to diagnose their illness and prescribe for it and they wouldn't be at all happy—or even alive for very long—with a doctor who summarized what medical science had discovered about their complaint and then told them to decide for themselves." —Dwight Macdonald, "Three Questions for Structural Linguists, Or Webster 3 Revisited," in *Dictionaries and That Dictionary* by James Sledd and Wilma R. Ebbitt (Chicago: Scott, Foresman and Company, 1962).

f. "Every other author may aspire to praise; the lexicographer can only hope to escape reproach, and even this negative recompense has been yet granted to very few." —Dr. Samuel Johnson.

31. Compare the following items and discuss their relationship to each other and to the W3 controversy.

a. From an editorial in a newspaper: "Our dictionaries, which used to be the greatest authorities of proper usage, have lowered their standards and now accept any kind of word as good English."

b. *Time* reports that Italian scholars are finally bringing out a comprehensive modern dictionary. Up to now, Italian dictionaries, controlled by purists who would not admit words which could not be found in medieval and renaissance literature, have been of little use to anyone seeking information about current Italian words.

32. Assume that you are a lexicographer and answer this statement: "Every good Kansan knows that the correct pronunciation of the river is the Ar·KAN′sas River. If those in Arkansas choose to mispronounce it as the AR′kan·saw River, that's their business, but they are wrong."

33. What variant pronunciations might you hear for *Oregon, Willamette* (a river in Oregon), *New Orleans, St. Louis, Illinois?* Are there any place names in your locality which have variant pronunciations?

34. Discuss how your language might vary in each of these situations: making a speech setting forth all of your qualifications for school office, applying for a job, talking to a friend about a date, writing an article for a magazine telling how you "modified" your stock car, talking with the family around the dinner table, writing a school constitution.

35. This dialog is from John Steinbeck's *The Grapes of Wrath:*

"I knowed you wasn't Oklahomy folks. You talk queer kinda— That ain't no blame, you understan'."

"Ever'body says words different," said Ivy, "Arkansas folks says 'em different, and Oklahomy folks says 'em different. And we seen a lady from Massachusetts, an' she said 'em differentest of all. Couldn't hardly make out what she was sayin'."

After reading the passage can you pick out words and usages which are substandard? Contrast the attitude toward pronunciation expressed here with that in question 32. What is wrong with substandard English? Does it fail to communicate? Does it create an impression about its user? Rephrase the passage in standard English.

36. Discuss: What is standard English? After your discussion, compare your conclusions with the definition of standard English in W3.

SPECIAL PROJECTS

1. Write definitions, suitable for dictionary use, of three slang terms in current use at your school.

2.   Pick out a word or meaning which is new to you and look for examples of its use in print. Each time that you see it, make out a citation slip for it, following the example given in this chapter. When you get seven or eight citations, write your definition for the word, basing it upon the meaning as revealed by the citations.

3.   As a group project, write a dictionary of useful terms for students in your school. Include a guide for pronunciation, definitions, verbal illustrations, labels, grammatical designations, and whatever other information you think will be useful.

4.   Using any of the following materials as sources, and others listed in the *Reader's Guide*, investigate the case for or against W3. The results may be used as materials for a composition or a panel discussion.

> "Sabotage in Springfield," *The Atlantic*, January 1962, pp. 73–77, written by Wilson Follett.

> "The String Untuned," *The New Yorker*, March 10, 1962, pp. 130–134, 137–140, 143–150, 153–160, written by Dwight Macdonald.

> "But What's a Dictionary For?" *The Atlantic*, May 1962, pp. 57–62, written by Bergen Evans.

> "The Lexicographer's Uneasy Chair," *College English*, May 1962, pp. 682–687, written by James Sledd.

> "Ruckus in the Reference Room," *Union College Symposium*, Spring 1962, pp. 3–9, written by Patrick E. Kilburn.

All these articles and many others relating to the topic can be found in *Dictionaries and That Dictionary* by James Sledd and Wilma R. Ebbitt (Chicago: Scott, Foresman and Company, 1962.)

9

Using a Dictionary

1. Content and Structure of the Dictionary

The dictionary stands ready to deliver more specific language information than most people expect of it. Spellings and meanings are always in demand by dictionary-users. But aside from these, the dictionary gives a variety of other linguistic data: for example, etymology (word origins), pronunciation, capitalization, usage, and rules of grammar.

In addition to this linguistic information most dictionaries contain several appendixes of miscellaneous matter. In a typical good desk dictionary, there may be from 40 to 50 pages of supplementary and explanatory material which the editors thought important to include. Each dictionary will vary somewhat in the kinds of information given, but usually it will include specific directions on the use of the book, convenient tables or outlines of useful knowledge, and special information about the English language. Some dictionaries incorporate entries relating to people and places (biographical and place names) into the main body of the text; others place them in special sections. Except for this distinction, the general formats are much alike.

Exercises

To get acquainted with the information the dictionary contains, try to find the answers to the following. They may appear in the main entry or in one of the supplements.

1. What is a *zeppelin* and why was it so named?
2. What does the symbol ⊕ stand for in astronomy?
3. Who was born later: Samuel Beckett or Thomas à Becket?
4. How is *Tanganyika* pronounced?
5. What are two reasons for capitalizing the word *Tabasco*?
6. Besides a cat, what else is a *tabby*?
7. Find an earlier meaning for the word *table* than "a flat piece of furniture set on legs."
8. What are the names of the Muses?
9. What was the mystery about Amelia Earhart?
10. What is the nickname of Huddle Ledbetter?
11. What is the Roman numeral for 500?
12. What is the proofreader's mark for *delete*?
13. What does the root *biblio-* mean as it appears in the word *bibliography*?
14. What is a *rinky-dink* and what usage label does it carry?
15. If you had a *rimple,* would you shoot it, iron it, or cook it?
16. How many colleges are in the Claremont Group?
17. What salutation should you use when you write to your senator?
18. What is the name of the ninth month in the Moslem calendar?
19. Which is longer, a nautical or a statute mile?
20. What does the footnote reference *cf* stand for?
21. What usage note does your dictionary attach to the word *somewheres*?

2. Using the "Table Alphabeticall"

Table Alphabeticall of Hard Words, the title of a very early English dictionary, reminds us that the dictionary is an alphabetical arrangement of words and that if we are to find words quickly in the dictionary when we need them, we must know how the system works. Alphabetizing is basically simple. Words beginning with the same letter are arranged together. They are, in turn, placed in alphabetical order determined by the second letter of the word. If the second letter is also the same, the order is determined by the third letter, and so on. Thus *construct, constructional, constructivism, constructor, construe* would appear in that order.

Here are some special considerations to keep in mind as you look for words:

1. Some words, although spelled alike, are different in meaning; in fact, they may have little relationship to each other beyond the accident of spelling. They will therefore appear consecutively as separate word entries. *Webster's Seventh New Collegiate*, for example, has three separate entries spelled *capital*, two spelled *pram*. In cases of duplicate spellings, be sure to read all entries carefully in order to select the right definitions.

2. *All* entries follow one another in alphabetical order, whether they be single letters (*G*), abbreviations, or acronyms (*G.I.*), combining forms (*gastro-*), or compounds (*girl Friday*). In the alphabetization of this last example, an open compound, you should think of it as being spelled as one word—*girlfriday*. The following entries would appear in your dictionary in this order: *G, gab, gaga, galley slave, gam, gamy, -gamy, G.I., girl Friday, girlish, G.O.P.*

3. Dictionaries differ about the alphabetical placement of proper names or derivatives of proper names which begin with *Mc* or *Mac*. *Webster's New World Dictionary* alphabetizes *McCoy* in its strict alphabetical place among the *Mc*'s. *Webster's Seventh New Collegiate* includes it under the *Mac*'s, treating it as though it were actually spelled that way, so that a reader uncertain of the spelling need look it up only once.

4. To help find entries alphabetically, dictionaries have head words in large dark type at the top of each page. At the top left column is printed the first entry word on the page. At the top right column is printed the last entry word on the page. Before you actually zero in on the word you want, it helps to flip the pages quickly, scanning the head words until you come to the page upon which your word should be located. Practice making use of head words as you look up entries. They cut down your looking time considerably.

Exercises

1. Arrange the following list of words in alphabetical order.

postmaster general	seacoast	ball bearing
A.A.	A.C.L.U.	monometer
ballistic missile	macaw	McCoy, the (real)
sea anchor	ballistics	manor
M.C.	man on horseback	A.A.A.
Amazon	sea bass	macaroni

172

Words, Words, Words: Vocabularies and Dictionaries

Last Judgment

subject label

pronunciation

derived terms

usage label

etymology

part of speech

during; durable; permanent; as, a *lasting* peace. *n.* 1. endurance; permanence. 2. a strong twilled cloth used for shoe uppers, covering buttons, etc.

Last Judgment, in *theology,* 1. the final judgment of mankind by God or Jesus, at the end of the world. 2. the time of this.

last·ly (last′li, läst′li), *adv.* in conclusion; finally.

last offices, final rites and prayers for a dead person.

last quarter, 1. the period when the moon's apparent shape is changing from half-moon to new moon. 2. the moon's apparent shape when this period begins.

last sleep, death.

last straw, [from the last straw that broke the back of the overburdened camel in the fable], the last of a sequence of annoyances or troubles that results in a breakdown, defeat, etc.

Last Supper, 1. the last supper eaten by Jesus with his disciples before the Crucifixion, on the night of his betrayal by Judas: cf. **Lord's Supper.** 2. a famous painting by Leonardo da Vinci depicting this supper.

last word, 1. the final word or speech, regarded as settling the argument. 2. something regarded as incapable of improvement. 3. [Colloq.], the very latest style, model, development, etc.

Las Ve·gas (läs vā′gəs), a city in southeastern Nevada: pop., 64,000.

lat (lät), *n.* [*pl.* LATS (läts), LATU (lä′too)], [Lett. *lats,* pl. *lati* < *Lat*via], former monetary unit of Latvia.

Lat., Latin.

lat., latitude.

La·ta·ki·a (lä′tä-kē′ä), *n.* 1. a district of Syria, on the Mediterranean: area, 2,800 sq. mi. 2. its capital, a seaport: pop., 59,000: ancient name, *Laodicea.* 3. (lat′ə-kē′ə), a fine grade of Turkish smoking tobacco: so called because produced near the port of Latakia.

latch (lach), *n.* [ME. *lacche* < *lacchen,* to seize, catch hold of; AS. *læccan, læccean*], 1. a fastening for a door or gate, especially one capable of being worked from either side by means of a lever and consisting of a bar that falls into a notch in a piece attached to the doorjamb or gatepost: sometimes said of a spring lock on a door. 2. a fastening for a window, etc. *v.t. & v.i.* [< the *n.*], to fasten or close with a latch. **latch on to,** [Slang], to get or obtain.

on the latch, fastened by the latch but not bolted.

latch·et (lach′it), *n.* [ME. *lachet;* OFr. *lachet,* dial. var. of *lacet,* dim. of *laz;* see LACE], [Archaic], a strap or lace for fastening a sandal or shoe to the foot.

From *Webster's New World Dictionary of the American Language,* college edition, copyright 1964 by the World Publishing Company, Cleveland, Ohio.

2. Which words in the following groups would be found on the pages covered by the head words?

Head Words	Entry Words
spiritless—spleen	spokesman, spongy, spittoon, splasher
exhibiter—exorbitant	exercise, existence, exhalant, exonerate
hither—hock	hitch, hockey, hobble, hives
horseman—host	Hosea, horse mackerel, hot, horticulture
piscatology—pitch	piston ring, pistol, piscivorous, pit
zeuxis—zoanthropy	zinc, Zeus, zodiac, zoo
scutellum—sea hog	scutellation, scythe, sea gull, seal

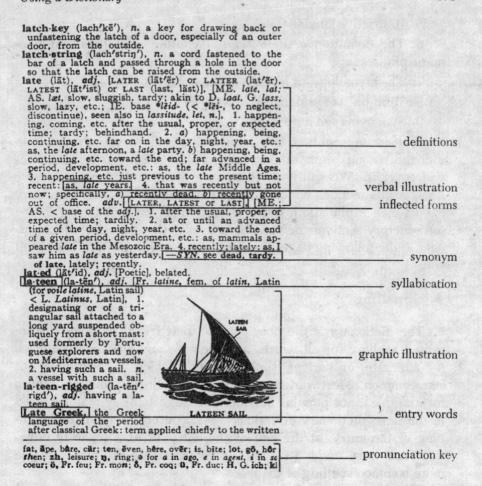

latch·key (lach′kē′), *n.* a key for drawing back or unfastening the latch of a door, especially of an outer door, from the outside.

latch·string (lach′striŋ′), *n.* a cord fastened to the bar of a latch and passed through a hole in the door so that the latch can be raised from the outside.

late (lāt), *adj.* [LATER (lāt′ēr) or LATTER (lat′ēr), LATEST (lāt′ist) or LAST (last, läst)], [ME. *late, lat;* AS. *læt,* slow, sluggish, tardy; akin to D. *laat,* G. *lass,* slow, lazy, etc.; IE. base *lēid-* (< *lēi-*, to neglect, discontinue), seen also in *lassitude, let, n.*], 1. happening, coming, etc. after the usual, proper, or expected time; tardy; behindhand. 2. *a)* happening, being, continuing, etc. far on in the day, night, year, etc.: as, the *late* afternoon, a *late* party. *b)* happening, being, continuing, etc. toward the end; far advanced in a period, development, etc.: as, the *late* Middle Ages. 3. happening, etc. just previous to the present time; recent: as, *late* years. 4. that was recently but not now; specifically, *a)* recently dead. *b)* recently gone out of office. *adv.* [LATER, LATEST or LAST], [ME.; AS. < base of the *adj.*], 1. after the usual, proper, or expected time; tardily. 2. at or until an advanced time of the day, night, year, etc. 3. toward the end of a given period, development, etc.: as, mammals appeared *late* in the Mesozoic Era. 4. recently; lately: as, I saw him as *late* as yesterday. —*SYN. see dead, tardy.* of late, lately; recently.

lat·ed (lāt′id), *adj.* [Poetic], belated.

la·teen (la-tēn′), *adj.* [Fr. *latine,* fem. of *latin,* Latin (for *voile latine,* Latin sail) < L. *Latinus,* Latin], 1. designating or of a triangular sail attached to a long yard suspended obliquely from a short mast: used formerly by Portuguese explorers and now on Mediterranean vessels. 2. having such a sail. *n.* a vessel with such a sail.

la·teen-rigged (la-tēn′-rigd′), *adj.* having a lateen sail.

Late Greek, the Greek language of the period after classical Greek: term applied chiefly to the written

LATEEN SAIL

— definitions
— verbal illustration
— inflected forms
— synonym
— syllabication
— graphic illustration
— entry words

fat, āpe, bâre, cär; ten, ēven, hēre, ōvēr; is, bīte; lot, gō, hôr then; zh, leisure; ŋ, ring; ə for *a* in *ago, e* in *agent, i* in *sa* coeur; ö, Fr. feu; Fr. mon; ô, Fr. coq; ü, Fr. duc; H, G. ich; kl

— pronunciation key

3. The Dictionary Entry

The heart of the dictionary is the entry. Here, within the few narrow-column lines of type, the important facts about a word are distilled. You can expect to find, when applicable, information about the following:

1. The standard spelling of the entry word (or words) and any variations, also its syllabication.

2. The pronunciation.

3. The part of speech.

4. The inflected forms of the word when they are formed irregularly.

5. Restrictive labels.

6. The definition or definitions, including subentries and idiomatic phrases.

7. The etymology, or history, of the word.

8. "Run-on" (or undefined derivative) entries.

9. Synonyms and antonyms.

The arrangement of this information will vary with the individual dictionary, but you may be sure that all standard dictionaries will cover it. We will have something to say about most of these items in the sections which follow. Remember that each dictionary has its own explanation, however, and that you will find it in the introductory section. Before doing any of the exercises which appear in the following pages, see what your own dictionary has to tell you.

4. Spelling

The dictionary is the poor speller's best friend. It gives the accepted spelling for all words, and includes any alternate spellings. An alternate, or *variant*, spelling is one which is acceptable but less common. Most variants are British spellings (*theatre, centre,* for example), not popular in American English. They may be listed in the same dictionary in various ways: consecutively at the beginning of the entry, at the end of the entry, or as a separate cross-reference entry under its own spelling, directing the reader to the more common spelling of the word.

The dictionary is also useful as a guide for spelling compound words. It is always a problem to know whether to use a hyphen, leave it out and spell the compound as two separate words, or run it together as one. For example, is it *boardwalk* or *board-walk, hovercraft* or *hover-craft, crosshatch* or *cross-hatch, double clutch* or *double-clutch?* Your dictionary will set a "style" for you—although another dictionary may disagree. Uniformity, rather than "correctness," must be the goal.

Exercises

1. Look up the section in your dictionary which discusses spelling. Does it say anything about preferred spellings? If it has a system of

indicating a preferred spelling, what is it? How does your dictionary present alternate spellings?

2. What alternate spellings does your dictionary give for the following words? You may have to read the whole entry carefully to find the information.

draft	dependence	bark	dialogue	pajamas
plow	traveled	czar	medieval	theater
curb	siphon	adviser	story	judgment

5. Pronunciation

A dictionary editor has two main duties to perform in dealing with pronunciation. First, he must decide exactly what the standard pronunciation is for each word. And if a word has more than one widely used pronunciation, he must be aware of this fact as well.

Second, he must record this information in such a way that the reader is able to interpret it quickly and correctly. Most dictionaries record the pronunciation immediately after the entry word. It is usually enclosed in parentheses (one dictionary uses slanted bars instead).

How do dictionaries record the pronunciation of a word? They differ to some degree on the markings and symbols which are used, but they all have these features in common:

1. The word is respelled phonetically so that the written symbols correspond as closely as possible to the sounds of the words.

2. Vowels are marked with special symbols when necessary to indicate that they are to be sounded in particular ways.

3. The word is divided into syllables, duplicating the syllable division which occurs when the word is spoken.

4. Accents, or vocal stresses that we may give certain syllables, are marked. Some dictionaries place the mark before the stressed syllable, and some place it after.

All dictionaries provide a special key to pronunciation in a place where it can be found easily, usually on the inside of the front cover or near it. They also reprint part of the key at the bottom of every other page throughout the book so that you can refer to it quickly.

In this section we would like to help you become familiar with a dictionary's pronunciation marking system and to give you practice in using it. For the sake of convenience we will use as our

example and guide the key from *Webster's New World Dictionary,*
reproduced here.[1]

Symbol	Key Words	Symbol	Key Words
a	fat, lap	b	bed, dub
ā	ape, date	d	did, had
â	bare, care	f	fall, off
ä	car, father	g	get, dog
e	ten, let	h	he, ahead
ē	even, meet	j	joy, jump
ê	here, dear	k	kill, bake
ēr	over, under	l	let, ball
i	is, hit	m	met, trim
ī	bite, mile	n	not, ton
o	lot, top	p	put, tap
ō	go, tone	r	red, dear
ô	horn, fork	s	sell, pass
o͞o	tool, troop	t	top, hat
oo	book, moor	v	vat, have
oi	oil, boy	w	will, always
ou	out, doubt	y	yet, yard
u	up, cut	z	zebra, haze
ū	use, cute	ch	chin, arch
ūr	fur, turn	ŋ	ring, drink
ə	a *in* ago	sh	she, dash
	e *in* agent	th	thin, truth
	i *in* sanity	*th*	then, father
	o *in* comply	zh	azure, leisure
	u *in* focus		

This dictionary, like others, indicates pronunciation by respelling
the word immediately after the entry word. Respelled words look
strange, but they help us sound out the word accurately. You can
expect changes like these:

1. A soft *c* becomes **s** as in *receive* (**ri-sēv'**).
2. A hard *c* becomes a **k** as in *card* (**kärd**).
3. A soft *g* becomes a **j** as in *gent* (**jent**).
4. The combination *ph* becomes **f** as in *phlox* (**floks**).
5. The combination *qu* becomes **kw** as in *quit* (**kwit**).

---

[1] From *Webster's New World Dictionary of the American Language*, College Edition,
Copyright 1966 by The World Publishing Company, Cleveland, Ohio.

6. The letter *x* becomes various letters, depending upon the word—*expect* (**ik-spekt′**), *exhibit* (**ig-zib′it**), *xylophone* (**zī′lə-fōn**).

7. Silent letters are omitted, so that *grille* becomes **gril**, *psychic* becomes **sī′kik**, and *choir* becomes **kwīr**.

The sounds which are assigned to the vowels and consonants are given in the pronunciation key. The consonant symbols require little explanation, with the exception of these few which you may not be aware of: ŋ indicates the back-tongue nasal sound in *sing* and *drink* as differentiated from the nasal sound in words like *no* and *neither;* **th** indicates the sound of the initial consonants in *thin* and *truth;* **th** indicates the sound of the initial consonants in *then* and *father;* zh represents the sound we make when we pronounce the *z* in *azure* and the *s* in *leisure*.

The vowel symbols, which are indicated in the left-hand column, need more explanation. Since each vowel letter can stand for more than one sound, some of them are differentiated by signs placed above the letter. These signs are called diacritical marks. *Webster's New World Dictionary* uses five diacritical marks and the schwa to indicate different vowel values.

The schwa differs from other marks in that it is a replacement for the vowel in phonetic spelling rather than a mark placed over a vowel. Its symbol (ə), which looks like an upside-down *e*, is being used by more and more dictionaries to represent the unstressed *uh* sounds which we get from the *a* in *ago*, the *e* in *agent*, the *i* in *sanity*, the *o* in *comply*, and the *u* in *focus*. Written phonetically with the schwa, these words would appear as **ə-go′**, **ā′jənt**, **san′ə-ti**, **kəm-plī′**, and **fō′kəs**.

The bar (–) or macron, indicates the sound of the vowel in words like *even* (**ē′vən**), *note* (**nōt**), *ice* (**īs**), *mate* (**māt**), and *use* (**ūz**). Vowels which are marked with the bar are pronounced just as they are when we name them as letters of the alphabet.

Vowels are unmarked in words like *that, men, miss, hot, took, boil, out,* and *rut*. Notice the difference in pronunciation between the unmarked vowel and the vowel marked with the bar: *cap* (**kap**)—*cape* (**kāp**), *bit* (**bit**)—*bite* (**bīt**), *cod* (**kod**)—*code* (**kōd**), *cut* (**kut**)—*cute* (**kūt**).

The double dot has two purposes. When it appears above the vowel ä like this, it denotes the sound of the vowel in *father* (**fä′thər**) and *calm* (**käm**). It is also used in the entry word (but not in the pronunciation respelling) to indicate that the second of two consecutive vowels is to be pronounced in a separate syllable, as in *naïve* and *coöperate*. This last use may be part of the common spelling of the word or an alternate spelling choice (see spellings of *cooperate* in your dictionary).

The wavy bar (*tilde*) is used over the vowel to indicate the sound heard in words like *river* (**riv′ẽr**) and *burn* (**bũrn**). The symbols **â, ê,** and **ô** are followed by *r*, and tell us how to pronounce the vowels in words such as *bare* (**bâr**), *here* (**hêr**), and *fork* (**fôrk**).

As part of their job of indicating pronunciation, dictionaries divide words into syllables, which are defined as "words or parts of words pronounced with a single vowel sound and one or more consonant sounds." Actually, dictionaries give us syllable divisions in two ways—division for writing, which is indicated in the entry word, and division for speech, which is indicated in the respelling for pronunciation. Words are not always divided the same way in these two places. For example:

Entry World Syllabication	Pronunciation Syllabication
ac·com·plice	ɔ-kom′ plis
ac·claim	ɔ-klām′
glis·sade	gli-säd′

Accent marks are used as a guide for pronunciation also. They show that stress is placed on a particular syllable of a word. Most dictionaries use a heavy accent mark (′) to indicate primary stress and a lighter mark (′) to indicate secondary stress. Syllables with no accent marks receive no stress. Notice these examples:

dif′er-ɔnt	**pur′s′nɔl**	(primary stress and no stress)
dif′ẽr-en′shɔl	**pur′sɔ-nal′ɔ-ti**	(secondary, primary, and no stress)

Note that in *different* and *personal* only the first syllable of each word is stressed. The second and third syllables are unstressed. In *differential* and *personality* two syllables of each word are stressed, but to different degrees. In each case, the heavier accent mark now appears over the third syllable and a lighter accent mark appears over the first syllable. This usage indicates that the stress shifted as syllables were added to the shorter words *different* and *personal.*

Many words of three syllables or more will contain primary stress, secondary stress, and no stress.

Do dictionaries ever indicate more than one pronunciation for a word? Yes. They give as many commonly accepted pronunciations as they conveniently can, usually with the most widely used pronunciation first. Most dictionaries, like *Webster's New World,* insist that the order in which alternate pronunciations is given does not necessarily indicate that one is preferred over another, "since all represent standard use." It was not always thus, however. In the past, many American dictionaries based their pronunciation upon the theory that each word had one standard pronunciation (largely the usage of New England) and that any deviation from that standard was incorrect. Students were being instructed only thirty years ago by their English teachers and by their dictionaries that the only correct pronunciation for *aunt* was **änt** and that the only acceptable pronunciation for *spectator* was with a stress on the second syllable (**spek-tā′tẽr**). This was hard advice to swallow for students living in a region where everyone (including the English teacher, in unguarded moments) was saying **ant** and **spek′tā-tẽr.** In fact, in some circles saying **änt** was "asking for a fat lip"! Today, almost everyone will agree that proper pronunciation is that which you feel comfortable using because it is the accepted pronunciation of your own region.

Exercises

1. Compare the symbols in your dictionary's pronunciation key with those of *Webster's New World Dictionary* presented at the beginning of this section. Note any differences.
2. Why do you think these differences exist?
3. Look up the following words in the dictionary; copy their phonetic respellings, taking care to place the bar (–) over the proper vowels.

braid	amalgamate	phoneme	final
utopia	realize	famous	steep
sheath	dismay	machine	brooch

4. Look up the following words and indicate on separate paper the vowel sounds represented by the schwa (ə). Substitute the schwa if you find that your dictionary uses a different symbol for the sound.

similar	holograph	opulence	pneumonia
vanity	common	effect	gossip
nauseous	passion	cadenza	instigate

5. Look up the following words in the dictionary, divide them by syllables as indicated in the pronunciation respelling, and place the accent marks where the stresses fall.

absenteeism	Altamira	editorial	plenipotentiary
photo	photograph	photography	extraordinary
formidable	congruent	decadence	antimony

6. Look up the following words in your dictionary, copy them with their phonetic markings on your paper, and be ready to pronounce them when called upon.

Antonia	badinage	concerto	Renaissance
blackguard	restaurant	apricot	pedometer
coupon	often	naive	indefatigable
inquiry	Sioux	Himalaya	Buenos Aires

7. Using the *Webster's New World* key as a guide, copy the following words and mark them for pronunciation as you think the editors of that dictionary would mark them. (You will also have to respell phonetically, divide into syllables when necessary, and indicate stress.)

alpine	enter	lope	family	measure
seat	mule	learn	stop	rover
mare	caper	jobber	kindle	mind

8. Look up the markings for the same words in your dictionary and compare the results.

9. The following words appear as they are marked for pronunciation in *Webster's New World Dictionary*. Using the pronunciation key as a guide, pronounce them in class.

inexorable (**in-ek′sĕr-ɔ-b′l**)

chaise (**shāz**)

minutiae (**mi-nū′shi-ē′**)

jeopardy (**jep′ĕr-di**)

dacron (**dā′kron**) (**dak′ron**)

depreciate (**di-prē′shi-āt′**)

dachshund (**däks'hoond'**) (**daks'hund'**) (**dash' hund'**)
  (**däkhs'hoont'**)

chassis (**shas'i**) (**shas'is**) (**chas'i**)

amateur (**am'ə-choor'**) (**am'ə-toor'**) (**am'ə-tyoor'**)

altimeter (**al-tim'ə-tẽr**) (**al'tə-mē'tẽr**)

Odysseus (**ō-dis'ūs**) (**ō-dis'i-əs**)

Oedipus (**ed'ə-pəs**) (**ē'də-pəs**)

aluminum (**ə-lōō'mi-nəm**)

(aluminium (Br.) (**al'yoo-min'i-əm**)

Mayan (**mä'yən**)

piety (**pī'ə-ti**)

epitome (**i-pit'ə-mi**)

barbarous (**bär'bə-rəs**)

deprecate (**dep'rə-kāt'**)

extremity (**iks-trem'ə-ti**)

10. Some words shift stress when used as different parts of speech. Indicate by an accent mark over the proper syllable the proper stress of each of these.

Verb	*Noun*
conduct	conduct
digest	digest
convict	convict
transfer	transfer
conflict	conflict

11. Does your dictionary list variant pronunciations for the following words? Look them up; copy the pronunciations given, and be ready to pronounce them when called upon. Which pronunciation do you normally use for each?

rodeo	harass	oblique	betroth
Oregon	chimpanzee	coupon	laboratory
gibber	opiate	tomato	aunt
schedule	isolation	creek	cigarette
library	catsup	vaudeville	automobile

12. The magazine *Literary Cavalcade* says that the following words are among the most often mispronounced words in the English language: *lamentable, incognito, culinary, gondola, conversant,*

bestial, impious, vacuum. Such lists seem to suggest that there is only one pronunciation for each word and that all dictionaries agree upon it. Are these notions true? Compare the listed pronunciations for the words in three or four dictionaries, including an unabridged, and report upon your findings. Are there any variants? Do any dictionaries differ?

13. How does your dictionary indicate the division of words by syllables? Look up the following words and write them as they are divided by syllables in (a) the entry word and (b) the phonetic transcription. Which division do we use in speech and which in writing? Be prepared to discuss your findings in class.

accord	desert (n.)	acquire	exhale	revival
accolade	desert (v.)	exercise	grinder	supplement
binder	dessert (n.)	exert	obliterate	vaccine

6. Parts of Speech and Inflected Forms of Words

Parts-of-speech labels are given for each grammatical use of a word in the dictionary entry. Definitions are arranged according to these labels, so that if one is looking for the uses of a particular word as a verb, for instance, he can scan those definitions which follow the verb label. Thus, in *Webster's New World Dictionary*, Second College Edition, the first fourteen definitions for the word *round* are listed after the label —*adj.* (adjective); the next fifteen are listed after the label —*n.* (noun); the next nine are listed after the label —*vt.* (verb transitive); the next four are listed after the label —*vi.* (verb intransitive); the next thirteen are listed after the label —*adv.* (adverb); and the next nine are listed under —*prep.* (preposition). Each definition is numbered, and the numbering begins anew following each part-of-speech label.

The dictionary gives information about the inflected forms of words as well. The *inflected forms* are those forms a word takes when it has undergone certain grammatical changes: for example, changes in nouns from singular to plural, changes in verb tense, and changes in the adjective and adverb to the comparative and superlative degrees. Dictionaries make it a point to list inflected forms when they are irregular—that is, when they are not formed by the simple additions of a suffix to the main entry. Thus, nouns which have irregular plurals (*hoof—hooves, child—children*), verbs which have irregular tenses (*begin—began, bring—brought*), and adverbs and adjectives which have irregular comparatives and superlatives (*well, better, best* and *little, less, least*) will be identified, and the irregular forms will be given right after the pronunciation of the word.

Exercises

1. Give the plural forms of the following words as you find them listed in the dictionary.

mosquito	mystery	nautilus	appendix
alumnus	beef	daughter-in-law	ox
politics	crisis	cargo	cupful

2. Using your dictionary, find and list the principal parts of these verbs:

swim	tear	draw	do	burst
drink	take	write	hang	go

3. Find in your dictionary and copy a verb and noun sense for each of these words:

throw	break	bank	treat

4. Find three words in the dictionary which have three grammatical designations each.

7.   Labels

One service that the dictionary performs for the reader is to tell him of the special ways in which some words are used. It does this by attaching labels to words. They may be status labels, regional labels, or subject labels.

The status labels that are generally used are these: *obsolete*, which refers to words no longer in use; *archaic*, which refers to words still in use but rarely used, since they are survivors of an earlier period; *colloquial*, which refers to words not normally used in formal communication but which are standard usage in informal writing or conversation; and *slang*, which refers to words used very informally and which are often considered to be nonstandard, though they are used by the best speakers. Words which are unlabeled are considered to be standard, formal English.

A regional label applied to a word implies that it is used chiefly in a certain part of the world or in a certain part of this country. The label may appear simply as *dialect*, or it may more specifically name the area in which the word is current, as in the label *British*.

Subject labels name the special field or subject in which a word has a particular meaning, as in astronomy, or physics, or religion.

Labeling is by no means uniform among dictionaries, since judgments may differ about the status of any word. Labels are not to be interpreted as an absolute dictum, but rather as an editor's helpful opinion about the current circumstances of the word.

Exercises

1. Look up the following words in your dictionary and list the labels, if any, which your dictionary has for any of the definitions:

betimes	knave	creep	rod	cracker
bloody	con	kirk	quoth	goon
nag (a person)	doc	bogie	margent	jack (money)
butterball	azimuth	gyre	gyp	gunwale
lateral	judgment	latent	yeah	yare
yap	xylene	y-	valid	utter

2. Look up the following words in your dictionary and list the British or Australian meaning for each:

lift	billabong	petrol	boot
swag	lorry	flat	public house
navvy	bobby	paddock	public school

3. Look up the following words in several dictionaries and list the dialect label for each word. If the dictionaries do not attach a specific regional dialect label, try to determine from the definitions what section of the country might use the word.

granny	chuck wagon	levee	jaybird
chaps	sharpie	cannikin	alamo
selectman	potlatch	cornpone	lightwood

8. The Definition

A good definition must be concise, accurate, and clear. It must be short enough to fit into the very small space allotted it, but it must be complete enough to satisfy the reader. It must also distinguish among the several related senses, or shades of meaning, and must present them in some kind of order, whether it be oldest meanings first or common meanings first.

Words are defined in more than one way; phrasal explanations, synonyms, illustrative sentences, and even pictures are used to make meanings clear. Writing a good definition is not easy, but there is a pattern of definition which fits some kinds of words. Both verbs and nouns can often be defined by more general words—infinitives and nouns to which limiting or distinguishing information is added, as in these examples:

Entry Word	General Word	Distinguishing Criteria
regale	to entertain	agreeably
riddle	a question or statement	so framed as to exercise one's ingenuity in answering it
wretch	a person	who is miserable or unhappy
wrestle	to struggle	hand to hand with an opponent

Ideally, a dictionary definition should not be phrased in words which in turn have to be looked up. This ideal is not easy to achieve with words having a narrow and highly technical meaning, however. For example, only a student of biology would be at home with this one—*delamination:* "gastrulation in which the endoderm is split off as a layer from the inner surface of the blastoderm and the archenteron is represented by the space between this endoderm and the yolk mass."

A word of warning: when looking up the definition of an unfamiliar word, be sure that the definition you choose fits the context you have in mind. Some dictionaries arrange definitions in order of historical development, with the oldest meanings coming first. Others arrange them according to frequency of use, with the most commonly used meanings coming first. Remember to look under the word class (noun, verb, and the like) that matches the class of the word you are checking.

Sometimes a main entry will be followed by a run-on entry, which is a word derived from the preceding word but so closely related that no definition is given. For example, the run-ons for the word *gate* could be *gateless, gatelike,* and *gateman.* Some dictionaries feel that including self-explanatory run-ons is mere space wasting, so they include only word derivatives which have developed special meanings. These are treated as separate entries.

Exercises

1. Look up the information in your dictionary relative to the arrangement of definitions within a word entry and be ready to explain it.
2. Where does your dictionary include the derivative entry *put on*—in a list of derivatives immediately following *put* or alphabetized in its regular place in the general word list?
3. Can you write a good definition? Here is another opportunity to express your thoughts precisely and accurately. If you are working on the assignment in the preceding chapter to collect citations for new words, perhaps you have enough evidence of the words' meanings by now to write definitions for them. Pick out a word of your own or choose from any of the following words, and write a clear and concise definition for it:

splashdown	syllable	scream	hippie	cool
groovy	skate	student	rock	chair

If a word has both a noun and verb meaning, write a definition for each. Compare your definitions with those of your classmates and with those found in dictionaries.

4. Which of these two groups of words have accumulated the most definitions?

    Group I: lie, house, man   *Group II:* recline, domicile, individual

How do you account for one group having more definitions than the other?

9. Etymology

Etymology is the origin and development of a word. Dictionaries give some of this information in very brief form in the part of the entry which is enclosed within brackets. It may be found either near the beginning or at the end of the entry, depending upon the dictionary. An etymology will usually tell in what period the word first appeared in English, what it meant, how it was spelled, what other languages it appeared in at that time, and, if it was borrowed, what languages it came from. To learn about the total development of a word's meaning, you will have to consider the definitions as well, since words continue to acquire meanings throughout their existence. Knowing what a word meant when it was created will not necessarily aid you in understanding its present meaning; in fact, the two may be quite different. Still, etymology has interest and value for its own sake. For further information, you are referred to Chapter 5, which treats the subject in more detail.

10. Synonyms

All crossword puzzle fans know that English is a language rich in synonyms—words which have nearly alike or closely related meanings in at least one of these senses. Listing synonyms for words is one of the helpful functions of the dictionary. Synonyms are found usually at the end of a word entry, often with an explanation of the precise differences in meaning between the synonyms and the word being defined.

Synonyms can be useful in two ways. First, they provide substitute words for you when you do not want to sound repetitious. Second, they can make your speech and writing more exact and interesting by giving you a choice of words with different shades of meaning. Often a synonym with the specific meaning that you need can be substituted for a more general word. Here, for example, are some synonyms for *cry*. They give you a variety of ways to talk about the act of crying.

Synonym	Discrimination of Sense
weep	stresses the shedding of tears
sob	to weep with a catch in the voice
whimper	to cry with low, whining, broken sounds
moan	a low, prolonged, mournful sound
blubber	used chiefly of children, implies a contortion of the face with weeping and broken, inarticulate speech
keen	a term used mostly by the Irish, means a wailing in lamentation for the dead

Synonyms, then, can be especially useful because they do *not* mean precisely the same thing as the words they are synonymous with. Here is another example of the way in which synonymous meanings are discriminated by the dictionary:

Synonym	Discrimination of Sense
combat	the most general of all these terms, means armed fighting without any other qualification
campaign	a series of military operations; it may involve a number of battles
battle	a large-scale, prolonged contest over a particular area
encounter	usually suggests a chance meeting of hostile forces
skirmish	a brief, light encounter between small units

People who use the language well use synonyms carefully. They choose the one which best carries the meaning to be conveyed.

You should remember that synonyms cannot always be used interchangeably for each other or for every sense of a word. *Furnish* is a synonym for one sense of the word *appoint*, as in "The office was well appointed." But you cannot use *furnish* in other senses of *appoint*, as in "I will furnish you to office."

Sometimes, one word in a group of synonyms will be more general in meaning than the others. *Cloister* is a general word which includes all these words in its meaning: *convent, nunnery, monastery, abbey,* and *priory.* They are all synonymous with *cloister,* but not all are synonymous with each other.

11.   Antonyms

An antonym is a word whose meaning is opposite to that of another word; examples are *sad—happy* and *dark—light.* It may be that most words do not have literal antonyms, or it may be that it is considered more useful to list synonymous words for us than words of opposite meaning. Whatever the reason, desk dictionaries list few antonyms.

Exercises

1. Dictionaries do not necessarily agree on the words for which synonyms will be listed. Check the following words in your dictionary. If synonyms are listed for them, write them down.

a. chief	f. skin	k. anger
b. choice	g. torment	l. appreciate
c. consent	h. amuse	m. appearance
d. contrary	i. defer	n. familiar
e. perplex	j. persecute	o. argument

2. Find and explain with the aid of your dictionary any distinctions in meaning among the words in any two of the following synonym sets:

a. beat, pound, thrash, flog.
b. caricature, parody, satire, burlesque.
c. break, smash, shatter, fracture.
d. bonus, bounty, premium, dividend.
e. fame, repute, notoriety, celebrity.
f. dainty, particular, fastidious, squeamish.
g. argot, slang, dialect, jargon.

3. Pick a set of synonyms from the following groups and use each synonym in a sentence designed to bring out its specific shade of meaning. You will need the help of your dictionary.

a. mob, horde, multitude, crowd.
b. dim, dusky, gloomy, murky.
c. deceased, defunct, extinct, inanimate.
d. copy, imitate, ape, emulate.
e. citizen, subject, native, national.

4. How far can you carry the search for the precise synonym? Is there only one good choice in the following sentences, or would you agree that several choices might fit in each sentence? Check these synonyms in your dictionary and discuss the suitability of each.

a. The horizon stretched before us in one _____, unbroken line.
　　(continual, continuous, constant, eternal, perpetual)
b. He was not a professional. He dabbled in the arts—collecting sculpture, attending exhibitions, and trying his hand at oils. He could be called a (an) _____.
　　(amateur, dilletante, novice, neophyte, tyro)
c. The dictator rode in a bulletproof car lest someone attempt to _____ him.
　　(kill, dispatch, assassinate, execute, murder)

d. She called for a witness in order to _____ her story.

   (confirm, substantiate, corroborate, authenticate, validate)

e. This paper is an exact _____ of the document, but reduced in size.

   (reproduction, facsimile, replica, copy)

f. The car, the first of a new kind, served as a (an) _____ for all which would be produced later.

   (example, pattern, paradigm, archetype, prototype)

Index

Index

NOTES